THE ROCKFORD PHILE

Behind-The-Scenes

The Unofficial Casebook of The Rockford Files

Designed and Edited by Hal Schuster

DAVID MARTINDALE is a former editor of The Houston Post and The Dallas Times Herald who now writes for publications including Premiere, Movie Marketplace, Inside Hollywood, The Armchair Detective, Video Marketplace and Tower Video Collector, as well as New Home Magazine, Writer's Digest, Ellery Queen's Mystery Magazine, Espionage Magazine, P.I. Magazine and Detective Story Magazine. His first book, to be released in February 1991, is Television Detective Shows of the 1970s: An Encyclopedia of Cops, Detectives, Lawyers and Sleuths.. He also writes a weekly sports trivia feature for a metropolitan daily newspaper.

THE ROCKFORD PHILE

Behind-The-Scenes

The Unofficial Casebook of The Rockford Files

By David Martindale

Books for the entertainment buyer

PIONEER

OTHER PIONEER BOOKS

•FISTS OF FURY: THE FILMS OF BRUCE LEE
Written by Edward Gross. March, 1990. $14.95, ISBN #1-55698-233-X
•WHO WAS THAT MASKED MAN?
Written by James Van Hise. March, 1990. $14.95, ISBN #1-55698-227-5
•PAUL MCCARTNEY: 20 YEARS ON HIS OWN
Written by Edward Gross. February, 1990. $9.95, ISBN #1-55698-263-1
•THE DARK SHADOWS TRIBUTE BOOK
Written by Edward Gross and James Van Hise. February, 1990. $14.95, ISBN#1-55698-234-8
•THE UNOFFICIAL TALE OF BEAUTY AND THE BEAST, 2nd Edition
Written by Edward Gross. $14.95, 164 pages, ISBN #1-55698-261-5
•TREK: THE LOST YEARS
Written by Edward Gross. $12.95, 128 pages, ISBN #1-55698-220-8
•THE TREK ENCYCLOPEDIA
Written by John Peel. $19.95, 368 pages, ISBN#1-55698-205-4
•HOW TO DRAW ART FOR COMIC BOOKS
Written by James Van Hise. $14.95, 160 pages, ISBN#1-55698-254-2
•THE TREK CREW BOOK
Written by James Van Hise. $9.95, 112 pages, ISBN#1-55698-256-9
•THE OFFICIAL PHANTOM SUNDAYS
Written by Lee Falk. $14.95, 128 pages, ISBN#1-55698-250-X
•THE MAKING OF THE NEXT GENERATION
Written by Edward Gross. $14.95, 128 pages, ISBN#1-55698-219-4
•THE MANDRAKE SUNDAYS
Written by Lee Falk. $12.95, 104 pages, ISBN#1-55698-216-X
•BATMANIA
Written by James Van Hise. $14.95, 176 pages, ISBN#1-55698-252-6
•GUNSMOKE
Written by John Peel. $14.95, 204 pages, ISBN#1-55698-221-6
•ELVIS-THE MOVIES: THE MAGIC LIVES ON
Written by Hal Schuster. $14.95, ISBN#1-55698-223-2
•STILL ODD AFTER ALL THESE YEARS: ODD COUPLE COMPANION.
Written by Edward Gross. $12.95, 132 pages, ISBN#1-55698-224-0
•SECRET FILE: THE UNOFFICIAL MAKING OF A WISEGUY
Written by Edward Gross. $14.95, 164 pages, ISBN#1-55698-261-5

Library of Congress Cataloging-in-Publication Data

1.   The Rockford Phile (television)

I. Title

Copyright © 1991 by Pioneer Books, Inc. All rights reserved.

Published by Pioneer Books, Inc., 5715 N. Balsam Rd., Las Vegas, NV, 89130.

Boxed: This publication is not licenced by, nor is Pioneer Books, affiliated with or Captital Cities/ABC Television Network Group, Stephen Cannell Productions or any other entity involved with the television series THE ROCKFORD FILES. THE ROCKFORD PHILE is a scholarly work intended to explore an American cultural phenemona and use of photos is for reference only with no infringement on the rights of the copyright holders intneded. THE ROCKFORD PHILE as a case study in the exploration of a cult television show.

Quotes attributed to specific periodicals are copyright by the respective publications cited.

ACKNOWLEDGEMENTS

I wish to express my sincerest gratitude to everyone who assisted me in the research and writing of this book.

Special thanks, of course, go to Rockford Files creators Stephen J. Cannell and Roy Huggins, executive producer Meta Rosenberg and co-stars Stuart Margolin and Joe Santos, all of whom were remarkably generous with their time and input.

Also assisting me in ways large or small were Jim Rondeau, Linda Stewart, Mark Baker, Celeste Williams, John Williams, Cinda Gillilan, Houston's KHTV (Channel 39) and the staff of the Orlando Public Library.

THE ROCKFORD PHILE

BACKGROUND

CHAPTER ONE:

THE HARD-LUCK P.I.

"This is Jim Rockford. At the tone leave your name and message. I'll get back to you."

That was the recording prospective clients heard when they dialed the number of James Scott Rockford—the most grossly underpaid and underappreciated private detective in the business.

Played by James Garner for six seasons on *The Rockford Files*, an endearingly popular series despite the fact that it ceased production more than a decade ago, Rockford also was one of the most unlikely heroes in the history of television.

He was a wise-cracking ex-con who served five years in San Quentin for a crime he didn't commit. When pardoned by the governor after new evidence cleared his name, he established his own one-man Los Angeles-based detective agency.

NO CRUSADING CRIMEFIGHTER

Make no mistake, though. Rockford was by no means a crusading crime fighter; a man selflessly dedicated to sparing others from the injustices he himself encountered.

Most television heroes with a checkered past like his might be inclined to become crusaders—but not Rockford.

He was just a working stiff—a guy trying his damnedest to eke out an honest living. He charged $200 a day plus expenses and specialized in cases left inactive by the police.

In the process he gave us a new and clearer vision of what being a private investigator is all about. After all, if *The Rockford Files* wasn't reality—and many real-life private investigators insist it wasn't—at least it felt that way.

"It's not like it is on TV," he once noted.

The almighty dollar, or the lack thereof, was constantly one of Rockford's primary concerns. He had trouble making ends meet. Bill collectors hounded him.

His office was a beat-up house trailer, parked on Malibu Beach. It was his home as well. "It's cheap, tax-deductible, earthquake-proof—and when I get a case out of town, I take it with me."

It also was "in hock up to its running lights."

Such factors were precisely what made him believable; he deviated from the standard TV detective profile in so many subtle ways.

Jim Rockford couldn't have been more different from, say, Joe Mannix, if he'd tried.

A NEW TWIST

Most TV detectives, for instance, were loners, with no family and few friends to speak of. Rockford had an abiding relationship with his father, a retired truck driver everyone knew as Rocky, and he had friends from all walks of life.

Most TV detectives had saucy secretaries minding the office, but not Rockford. All he had to take his incoming calls was that blasted tape machine.

Most TV detectives had carte blanche at the local police department, pooling information with the cops, occasionally even working together with them as a team. Not so with Rockford. Aside from Sergeant Dennis Becker of the LAPD, the one officer who put up with our hero, Rockford got nothing from cops but grief.

Where most TV detectives were like rock-solid Timexes—they took a licking and kept on ticking—Rockford was decidedly more human. "I bruise easy."

Did he ever. When thugs belted him, he went down—hard! And when he got up again, he moved a great deal more slowly.

And when Rockford threw the punch? He was as liable as not to break his hand in the process.

THE CHARLIE BROWN P.I.

In short, *The Rockford Files* put a refreshing new twist on a familiar, at times even tired, formula.

This exchange between Rockford and a woman client, for instance, said it all:

"If that man hadn't tried to kill me today—"

"Wait a minute," said Rockford. "Wait a minute."

"What?"

"Who tried to kill you? Why didn't you tell me?"

"Physical violence has a tendency to put some people off."

"Yeah, I'm one of them. What happens when somebody decides to take another crack at you?"

"They won't. The attempt this morning was against a woman—alone and unarmed."

"And the next time it will be against the two of us—alone and unarmed."

"You're not armed?"

"No."

"But you're a private investigator. Why don't you carry a gun?"

"Because I don't want to shoot anybody."

A TV detective with an aversion to gunplay? You bet Jim Rockford was different.

If it was a hard-boiled detective you wanted, you simply would have to try another channel—for the hardest thing about Rockford was his luck.

Scarcely an episode passed without his being shot at, beaten up or thrown in Jail. And his seemingly lucrative pay rate, two hundred a day, wasn't all that impressive either.

"It's Just a little less than a good plumber will make if he doesn't work weekends," Rockford was quick to point out.

"And that's not day in and day out. I mean, there's actual days—weeks—I'm standing in the unemployment line."

Furthermore, most clients stiffed Rockford for his hard-earned fees anyway.

Simply put, Jim Rockford was a loser; the Charlie Brown of TV P.I.s.

His cases almost always wound up more complicated, more dangerous than he bargained for—and all because his clients lied to him, withheld information, scammed him, sometimes even set him up to be a fall guy for the cops or the mob.

HELP FROM HIS FRIENDS?

With friends like Rockford had, there was never a need for enemies.

Low-life con artist Angel Martin, for instance, Rockford's former San Quentin cellmate, was forever getting our hero in sticky situations. Whenever his harebrained scams and half-baked swindles went haywire, Angel would turn up on Rockford's doorstep, pleading for help.

Sometimes Angel would even implicate "Jimmy" in his shenanigans—without Rockford's knowledge, naturally—simply to get out of a Jam.

Angel: "You wouldn't shoot me for a lousy $100, would you?"

Rockford: "I ought to do it on general principles."

Over the years Rockford was double-crossed by former prison mates, ex-girlfriends, old Korean War buddies, childhood companions. From time to time even mush-minded Rocky was the unwitting source of headaches.

Lucky thing for Rockford he had a good head on his shoulders, one friend at the police department and a sharp lady lawyer (Beth Davenport) to bail him out of Jail.

Luckier still that he could handle his car, a gold Pontiac Firebird, like a professional stunt driver, for hardly an episode passed without a tire-squealing, gravel-spitting car chase in which Rockford pursued a bad guy or, even more likely, fled from one.

A PRACTICAL MAN

Rockford, after all, had a yellow streak a mile wide. As he saw it, there simply was no point in asking for trouble.

He already had all he could handle.

That is why he preferred to dabble in cases labeled closed by the police; he wouldn't have to cross paths with belligerent cops. That was why he didn't hire out as muscle; he disliked being shot at and beaten up.

Did that make him a coward?

"Well, of course," he once confessed. "That goes without saying."

But truth be told, there was more to him than that.

Like another memorable character James Garner played on television, the role that made him famous in fact, Jim Rockford wasn't afraid. Just infinitely practical.

Indeed, *The Rockford Files* has often been dubbed a "modern-day Maverick"—in reference to Garner's first TV series—and with good reason. For three years, from 1957 to 1960, Garner helped turn the TV Western formula on its ear with his portrayal of Bret Maverick, a cardsharp con artist who was downright inept with a gun but delightfully quick with his wits.

What made Maverick distinctive, in an era during which as many as 31 Westerns flooded the airwaves, was its offbeat, tongue-in-cheek sense of humor. It managed to turn the cliches of the traditional TV Western topsy-turvy, but without crossing too far into the absurd.

Maverick worked on two levels: It was a rousing action- adventure series—and a good-natured parody of same.

The same was true for *The Rockford Files*, which dismantled TV detective shows the way Maverick had Westerns.

As Garner once observed: "Jim Rockford was no less macho than anybody else. He Just did it in a different way. If you go back and look, when Maverick originally came on the air, there were 17 Westerns and the heroes in every one of them were steely-eyed and strong and brave.

"And Maverick came and said, 'Wait, don't (hurt me),' stuck his tongue in his cheek—and that was the end of the Western because we kind of punched holes in the balloon.

"You take Rockford, we did the same thing. There were how many detective shows on the air then? Twelve? And we came on and said. "No, no, no. You don't (have to) be that brave. That's not right.' And it kind of stopped those too.

"So we punched holes in a lot of balloons."

UNIQUELY ROCKFORD

The Rockford Files did so, however, not in a self-indulgently farcical way, as *Moonlighting* did a decade later, but in a far more subtle manner.

Who, other than Rockford, could become involved in a murder plot merely because a thug phoned death threats to his number by mistake?

13

Who else but Rockford could find himself in hot water with cops, crooks and clients alike, just because a blundering would-be P.I. had, by chance, been passing himself off as Jim Rockford to drum up some business?

Who but Rockford, after having car trouble in a small desert town, could bank $10,000 of his client's bail money in a real estate company's safe—only to have the cash turn up missing the following morning?

Who but Rockford could wind up in Dutch with jewel thieves after his barbecue pit, where the crooks happened to stash a stolen diamond, was ripped off by passing tourists?

And who but Rockford could find himself a target of the mob merely because a murder victim friend had mailed him a wheel of cheese shortly before dying?

Rockford was a loser, all right. (Perhaps there was something to the fact his series made its debut Sept. 13, 1974—Friday the Thirteenth.)

But a more likeable loser there never was.

After all, Rockford had a sense of humor and we loved him for it. We never pitied him simply because he accepted his misfortunes with a shrug and went on with his life.

This perhaps was never more evident than in Rockford's initial episode, in which Jim was grazed by a bad guy's bullet:

Rocky: "Two inches to the right and you might be missing that eye."

Rockford: "Look at it this way. Two inches to the left and it would have missed me completely."

Now that's looking on the bright side.

And what got lost in the shuffle, amidst all the action and all the laughs, was the fact that in spite of his hard luck, Rockford was very good at his job.

It was never easy, mind you, but he always unraveled the mystery at hand and caught the bad guy before the final credits rolled.

So what if he got screwed out of the credit for solving the case? So what if he got roughed up in the process? And so what if he didn't get paid afterward?

In the topsy-turvy world of Jim Rockford, one simply couldn't take matters such as those very seriously.

Mariette Hartley
and James Garner

CHAPTER TWO:

THE MAVERICK CONNECTION

Jim Rockford's father was a retired truck driver.

His grandfather? "As a matter of fact," Rockford once noted, "he was a horse thief."

And his great-grandfather? Why, he must have been none other than Bret Maverick.

Granted, there's absolutely no evidence to substantiate such a claim, no documentation to confirm any family ties, no explanation why Jim and his father Rocky no longer bear the Maverick name. The shows in which they starred, in fact, even appeared on rival networks, but if we explore Jim Rockford's roots, Bret Maverick without question commands a vitally significant role.

ROCKFORD'S ROOTS

If there never had been a Maverick, we likely would never have seen *The Rockford Files* either.

Rockford was introduced as television's most engaging private investigator March 27, 1974, when NBC telecast the series pilot. The origin of *The Rockford Files*, however, goes back much further than that—to an era in which cowboys, not cops, were king.

The year was 1957 and Westerns littered the airwaves. Marshal Matt Dillon and *Gunsmoke* topped the Nielsen ratings. Other TV heroes in the top 10 were Jim Hardie (*Tales of Wells Fargo*), Paladin (*Have Gun Will Travel*), Marshal Wyatt Earp (*The Life and Legend of Wyatt Earp*) and Vint Bonner (*The Restless Gun*).

All were straight-laced, laconic good guys. With the exception of Paladin, the suavely cultured gun for hire, they also were interchangeably emotionless automatons, so stiff they could pass for wooden Indians.

Then Bret Maverick and his brother Bart, a couple of smooth-as-silk gamblers, rode into town.

An unheralded but affable actor by the name of James Garner played Bret. Jack Kelly was Bart.

Something was undeniably different about the Maverick boys. When it came to the "code of the West," they apparently never found the playbook.

BREAKING THE RULES

As Maverick creator Roy Huggins put it: "What we set out to do was create a character that deliberately broke all the rules of the traditional Western hero."

That they did.

"He's the kind of guy who could have a love affair with a girl," Huggins said of his creation, "and then turn around and turn her in for a reward.

"And then, when the sheriff, who's thoroughly disgusted by Maverick's actions says 'Take your money and get out of town: you've got five minutes,' Maverick comes back at him with a wisecrack. He says, 'A town this size I can get out of in three.'

"That's Maverick, all right, a totally self-centered, self- serving individual."

Indeed, the Maverick brothers looked out only for themselves. They roamed from town to town, not in pursuit of bandits, but of high-stakes card games. They placed a premium on money, not honor. In the face of danger, they fled. If no escape was readily available, they wormed their way out of trouble with con-man quick wits and some mighty fast talking.

Whether they were yellow through and through—as they freely admitted—or merely practical was strictly a matter of opinion.

As for the tried-and-true Old West gunfight; well, that was never an option in the Mavericks' book, either. For neither could so much as hit the side of barn, even if they tried.

As Bart once put it: "I've got a brother who can outdraw me any time he wants to, and he's known as the second-slowest gun in the West."

TWISTING TALES

Bret and Bart usually alternated as leads—Huggins' way of stepping up the series' production process, filming two episodes in the time that only one normally could be shot—but the duo occasionally shared the screen.

Their travels took them to such improbably named towns as Hounddog, Bent Forks, Broken Wheel and Duck 'n Shoot. Their adventures, meanwhile, included out-and-out parodies of other TV shows, such as *Dragnet*, *Gunsmoke* and *Bonanza*.

The *Dragnet* send-up featured Joe Friday-like narration from Bret. The *Gunsmoke* episode, titled *Gun-shy*, pitted Bret against Marshal Mort Dooley, his lame deputy Clyde and Miss Amy of the Weeping Willow Saloon. In *Three Queens Full,Bonanza* send-up, Bart encountered Joe Wheelwright of the Subrosa Ranch and his dunderheaded offspring, Henry, Moose and Small Paul.

The quintessential *Maverick*, meanwhile, made an unwilling sheriff of Bret Maverick. "I'm unreliable," he said when pressured into accepting the Job. "I'm a terrible shot. And—I mean this most sincerely—I have been, for as long as I can remember, a coward."

When his protests went unheeded, Bret proceeded to demonstrate the Maverick method of law enforcement:

Need a safer way of dealing with a rowdy, gun-toting cowhand? Do like Maverick and challenge him to a hand of poker. (The rules were as follows: If the cowpoke won, he had carte blanche to plunder the town for the entire day, no reprisals. If Maverick won, it would be a day in jail for the loser.)

Need to break up a barroom brawl? Wager on one of the brawlers. (When Maverick did it, everyone eventually quit fighting, unwilling to help the sheriff turn a nifty profit.)

Need to stymie an impending bank robbery? Steal the money before the bandits strike, then bury the cash safely somewhere on the outskirts of town.

Such nonsense was par for the course on *Maverick*.

A SENSE OF HUMOR

In short, what this series had that its fellow oaters sorely lacked was a sense of playfulness. a sense of humor.

Or as Huggins put it: "What we did was an anti-Western. Once we went three episodes without

18

using so much as a gun or a horse."

That offbeat sense of humor, that refusal to take itself so seriously, was the secret to *Maverick*'s success.

And Huggins was quick to explain that success was no accident.

"There's a misconception about the early days of *Maverick*," said Huggins. who produced the series its first two years and wrote virtually every episode during that span. "That 'beady little eyes' story, the one where we 'switched' to comedy, isn't the way it happened at all."

The story to which Huggins referred—it's something of a television legend by now—goes that early in the first season, a bored scriptwriter's stage directions instructed Garner to look at someone "with his beady little eyes." The story continues that Garner, amused by the notion, played the scene, which was supposed to be straight, for laughs.

Garner's playfulness the legend then has it, turned *Maverick* into a tongue-in-cheek classic.

Not so, said Huggins.

"That's the story that ran in *TV Guide* during our second season," he said. "But *Maverick* was always an anti-Western. We didn't 'switch' to comedy. Just look at the first episode and you can see for yourself."

To the contrary, Huggins said, in the beginning the show's tongue-in-cheek formula was lost even on young Garner.

"In the third episode, we had a director (Budd Boetticker) who, with Garner's full permission, took all of Maverick's funny lines and gave them to another character, then gave Garner all the straight lines. It was all backwards, simply because this director—who's a very fine director, an amateur—didn't get it. He was accustomed to strong heroes in the Western mold.

"But Garner didn't do a thing to stop him. I had to sit him down and explain it to him. 'You gave away all the funny lines. Don't ever do it again.' And, to his credit, he never did.

"I'm not saying this to belittle Jim's contributions to the show, mind you. I mean, it wouldn't have worked without him. I picked him for the part. I recognized that he had a talent for playing that type of character and built a show around him."

And it was that same talent for playing anti-heroes that, years later, made *The Rockford Files* equally as memorable.

In the decades since his departure from *Maverick* in 1960, James Garner has steadfastly maintained that likeable, self- deprecating persona he first cultivated as Bret Maverick.

In fact, he's made a career out of it.

DEEPER CONNECTIONS

Jim Rockford likely would have had Maverick-like, anti-hero qualities no matter what—simply because the Maverick touch and the Garner touch were, for the most part, one and the same.

Yet the Maverick connection goes deeper than that.

"It was no accident," Huggins said. "It was quite deliberate that Rockford and Maverick were alike. It was cause and effect."

After Garner's rocky return to series television in 1971's *Nichols*, Huggins said, Garner got word to Huggins that he was eager to do another show.

"I didn't want to do another Western," Huggins said. "So I sat down and came up with a contemporary Western—with Maverick as a P.I. The two are so much alike because Maverick and Rockford are the same guy, just in a different setting."

Granted, *The Rockford Files* never offered us out-and-out parodies of rival detective shows as *Maverick* had with other Westerns. Yet, the new series smacked of the same inspired looniness.

The parodies were there, all right, just not quite so bluntly obvious this time around.

There was, for example, Lance White, the suavely polished private eye. Played to perfection—literally—by Tom Selleck, Lance could do no wrong: He was rich. He was handsome. He drove a fancy car, wore elegant clothes. He knew all the right people, attended all the right parties.

In short, he was perfect; aggravatingly so—precisely the way Amos Burke had been in his heyday, the way Thomas Banacek had been in his.

Lance White's character didn't poke fun at any one TV detective in particular. Instead, he satirized the entire genre of Mr. Perfect P.I.s, a type that goes as far back, in fact, as Dashiell Hammett's Nick Charles.

And the same was true of other offbeat sleuths who crossed paths with Rockford.

There was Freddie Beamer (played by James Whitmore Jr.), a nerdy garage mechanic—complete with thick eyeglasses, held together at the bridge with tape—who longed to become a hard-boiled detective.

There was Vernon St. Cloud (played by Simon Oakland), the poster child of sleazeball P.I.s.

And, of course, there was Richie Brockleman (played by Dennis Dugan), the 23-year-old gumshoe who looked like he belonged in junior college. ("Everyone underestimates me," Richie once said. "I count on it.")

All were richly humorous send-ups of TV detective types.

But those characters made their appearances during the series' later years, long after Huggins ended his involvement with the show.

MAVERICK=ROCKFORD?

Where the Maverick connection was most obvious—indeed, most significant—was in its lead character.

Like Bret Maverick, Rockford was something of a coward. He was forever trying to steer clear of cases in which he might be placed in danger. "I get myself messed up in an LAPD active file and I get my can shot off, my license pulled and probably get booked for obstructing justice."

Like Maverick, money, not honor, was his primary motivation in life. Rockford, for instance, never missed a chance to bring up his fee—"$200 a day, plus expenses"—a line which over the years became permanently lodged in our memories.

Also like Maverick, Rockford didn't like resorting to gunplay. "I don't shoot it," he once explained while digging a gun out of a coffee pot, where he often kept it buried up to the hammer. "I just point it."

Most especially like Maverick, Rockford was a grade-A schemer—a more-or-less good guy who happened to have larceny in his heart.

Over the years Rockford engineered some of the sweetest scams in the history of television, usually at the expense of con artists who had crossed him by bilking his friends. But, more important-

ly, Rockford's con-artist savvy proved infinitely valuable in the everyday execution of his job.

Rockford, for instance, had more aliases than most criminals. One of his favorites was Jimmy Joe Meeker, Oklahoma oilman. Other bogus identities included Jim Rockford, Double A Real Estate; Carter Simpson, assistant dean of admissions, Mollar Medical School; Jim Taggart, Department of Human Resources; Jim Slauson, Los Angeles County Medical Examiner, and Larry Metcalf, insurance adjuster, Great Western Casualties.

In fact, he kept a small offset press in the back seat of his car, just in case he needed a spur-of-the-moment fake business card.

And even in the face of danger, he never completely came clean. ("Okay, pal," he once told a masked gunman, "you've forced me to blow my cover—I'm a federal narc.")

Asked to provide his rationale behind this endless use of aliases, Rockford explained it this way:

"I took the name Metcalf for a wife-and-child abandonment case. I posed as an insurance adjuster. If I tell people that I'm dogging a wayward spouse, they think I'm a heel and lie through their teeth. But if they think I'm helping someone come into an unexpected fortune, they'll finger the poor slob every time."

CONFIDENCE MAN

Indeed, it was a lucky thing for the rest of the world that Rockford was, even if only in his own twisted way, a good guy. He would have made an outstanding confidence man.

Here, for instance, is a classic example of the master at his fast-talking best, a phony phone call in which Rockford set out to obtain a record of a pharmaceutical salesman's recent long-distance calls:

Rockford: "Hi, hon. Gene Creekmore (here)."

Operator: "What can I do for you, Mr. Creekmore?"

Rockford: "Well, I hope you can save my neck. You see. my company ships on bills of lading that are computer coded to the customer's P.O. number and then cross-coded to the billing address' telephone number. Can't be too careful when you're dealing in pharmaceutical."

20

Operator: "What can I do for you, Mr. Creekmore?"

Rockford: "Well, I lost my phone book, I did. And I had to call in to Pastoria an order from memory and I must have missed the number because the computer punched out the bill of lading but it kicks back the invoice every time. There's oxydinaphenamomitol lost in the shuffle and there's just no way for me to trace it unless I get the number, which I can't do without my phone book."

Operator: "Well, what can I do for you, Mr. Creekmore?"

Rockford: "Well, all I need is the telephone numbers that I called on Tuesday night. I'll hold while you get them off my bill."

Meanwhile, as Rockford waits for the information he requested, his father, who overheard the conversation, echoes our own sentiments exactly

"Man," Rocky marvels, "I don't know why you're not in more trouble than you're in!"

Still, Rockford persisted in doing things his way, the Maverick way.

Once, in fact, when a client protested his misrepresenting himself to gather information, insisting the best way is simply to "go in straight," Rockford was unable to conceal his disappointment

"But that takes all the fun out of it."

And that, in a nutshell, was why we loved Rockford.

His way might not have been the conventional way, the way other TV detectives did business—but still we wouldn't have had him any other way.

After all, if we took the Maverick out of Jim Rockford, we'd be taking all the fun out of him as well.

CHAPTER THREE:

THE BIRTH OF A NOTION

Robert Blake as Jim Rockford?

True, it's difficult to imagine such an improbable stroke of casting—but it could have happened.

Blake, perhaps best known for his role as the title character of the cop show *Baretta*, was Universal Studios' first choice to star in *The Rockford Files*.

How James Garner landed the role—indeed, how the series came into existence at all—was as improbable a set of circumstances as ever played out in any of the show's wilder story lines.

STARTING WITH A STRIKE

Simply put, a three-and-a-half-month strike by television writers ultimately led to the birth of Jim Rockford. A script that one network wouldn't touch with a 10-foot pole eventually resulted in one of the most memorable detective shows in the history of television.

The writers' strike of 1973 was the first ingredient. Pre-production for series premiering in September typically began half a year earlier, in March, with filming getting under way by June.

The strike, however, lasted into June before reaching a settlement, making a shambles of the usual timetable. As the networks were reluctant to back up their planned September-October premieres, writers and production crews had to scramble to meet deadlines.

From that crazy, whirlwind summer, Jim Rockford was created out of necessity.

The series Roy Huggins and Stephen J. Cannell were working on at the time was *Toma*, a detective series starring Tony Musante as a master-of-disguise undercover cop. The show was based on the real-life exploits of David Toma, a Newark, N.J., detective. Huggins was the series' executive producer; Cannell, its producer and top writer.

"It wasn't long before we realized the fifth episode wasn't going to be ready in time," Cannell recalled. "It still was going to be in the lab when it needed to be on the air—and you really don't want to rerun your first episode just five weeks into the season.

"So we went to ABC—me, Roy and Jo Swerling—and told them we won't have the fifth Toma in time. Can they schedule a pre- emption? They said no. They had already burned off everything they had stockpiled because of the strike.

"So we went to Universal and told them we had this problem. They said they'd never missed a deadline with an episode before and didn't want to miss one now.

"There didn't seem to be any answer."

But there was one—a notion that was remarkably simple yet fiendishly ingenious.

YOUR OWN PRE-EMPTION

"Roy came up with an idea." Cannell said. "He said, 'Why don't we create our own pre-emption?'

"This was the plan: Toma would have this suspicious death he was looking into—and he'd think he had a pretty good murder case. But when he'd take it to Spooner (Toma's boss, played by Simon Oakland), Spooner would say, "There's nothing here. This isn't a murder.' And he'd close the case.

"But Toma wouldn't let it rest. He'd feel so strongly about it that he'd take it to this private detective, Jim Rockford, who only does closed cases, and he'd say, 'Here.' Then Rockford would do the hour and at the end Toma would come in and say, Good job, Jim.'

"That meant we'd need Tony for only two scenes, the first and the last, and that way we could shoot it simultaneously with another Toma and gain ourselves a week."

That was the plan anyway.

No one at ABC or Universal objected to Huggins' innovative strategy. No one demanded to see a script right away either.

"Nobody much cared as long as we had something," Dannell said. "After all it was better than running a test pattern."

It was decided that the script would be written from a story Huggins had been "kicking around" for a time.

Then they came up with the name, Jim Rockford, by thumbing through a telephone directory of Universal employees.

"Roy opened up the phone book," Cannell said, "and picked a name. It was Bill Rockford or Tom Rockford, somebody Rockford, and that was that."

(Cannell's original script, in fact, called for the character to be named Tom Rockford. It was changed to Jim months later, after Garner had been signed to play the part.)

With the story and the lead character now roughed out, Cannell quickly went to work. Time was of the essence. He would have no more than 10 days to complete the script.

"I needed to write it really quick because for this plan to work we had to shoot it immediately. Nobody really cared what it was about.

"So I decided—why not have fun with it?"

Have fun with it he did.

BREAKING THE RULES

Cannell, a longtime mystery buff and particularly a fan of hard-boiled detective fiction, by writers such as Dashiell Hammett and Raymond Chandler, knew the genre like the back of his hand. He knew the rules—and just as Huggins had broken the rules years earlier when he created *Maverick*, Dannell broke the rules with Jim Rockford.

"But don't misunderstand me. I had no idea Jim Garner would wind up playing Rockford. I wasn't trying to do Maverick as a P.I. It just worked out that way later. I was working so fast I didn't even have time to think about it.

"I had no one in mind. Rockford was just a character I was writing."

Huggins, it must be noted, maintains he visualized the character as "a contemporary Maverick" from the very beginning, something tailored specifically for Garner.

No matter. The fact remains that Cannell would have to work as quickly as possible and both men put a high premium on breaking the rules.

Rockford certainly broke rules.

Said Cannell: "It was funny to have this . . . P.I. who'd react in certain situations, not the way a traditional private eye might, but the way any real person would.

"I mean, if somebody pulled a gun on Joe Mannix, he'd probably say something like, 'You better drop that gun or I'll break your arm.' And then he'd make good on the promise. That's the way P.I.s were on television.

"Now if somebody pulled a gun on me, I'd probably say something like, 'Here's my watch and my wallet. Don't hurt me.' And that's what I did with Rockford. Every time somebody threw a punch at him or took a shot at him, he'd chicken out and pull off the case."

Cannell wasn't content to stop with a cowardly hero, however. He found that toying around with the genre was entirely too much fun.

One significant influence for Dannell, for instance, was an episode of Mannix he had seen shortly before beginning work on the script. In that episode, rough-and-tumble Mannix agreed to look for a youngster's missing mother. His pay? Three dollars, some pennies and a lollypop.

"All these other P.I.s on TV, they never seemed to care if they got paid. Well, my guy would be the opposite. He'd run credit checks on his client before taking a case. He'd take the pink slip in lieu of payment. He'd itemize every little expense he could think of—stuff like, 'I'm charging you for gas for the one- point-seven miles I drove, but I'm not charging you for the wear and tear on my tires when I peeled rubber.'"

Instead of 10 days, Cannell needed only five.

"I laughed all the way through it " he said. "It was one of the best things I'd ever written. It's still one of the best things I've ever written."

PROBLEMS

There were new problems, however.

For starters, the script was much too long, 97 pages. For an hour-long episode, 60 pages would have been more like it. More damning, though, was the fact that ABC wouldn't touch it.

"Roy read it and he absolutely loved it. He called me up at night—after he'd finished reading it—and said, 'We're not changing a word.' "

Which is why the emergency Toma script Dannell had worked so feverishly to prepare never saw the light of day—not as a Toma episode, anyway.

"ABC hated it," Cannell said, "Just hated it. They said to 'cut all the junk out of it.'"

That "junk" happened to be the quirky touches that made Rockford so memorable in the first place.

"They said you can't do this on TV. A P.I. who quits every time he's threatened, running credit checks on his clients? The network just didn't want any of that.

"I suppose we could have cut it. It wasn't a bad mystery. But it would have been just an ordinary hour. And Roy—who was the quarterback of the whole thing at this point—said no way. So that was the end of that plan.

"It turned out that ABC wound up repeating the first Toma early anyway."

But Cannell and Huggins' efforts weren't exactly for naught.

Since the script wouldn't be used on Toma and since its length was more suited for ninety-minute movie treatment anyway, Huggins and Cannell began to explore other possibilities.

A movie pilot, perhaps?

"We took it to Universal," Cannell said "and they read it and said, 'It's a funny script' and all. 'But it needs something.' "

By "special" Universal executives actually meant "gimmick."

GIMMICKS

Gimmick detectives were the rage of the mid-'70s. There was Barnaby Jones, the old detective. There was Cannon, the fat detective. Ironside did his sleuthing from a wheelchair. Universal executives even offered, as an example, Longstreet, a short-lived series that featured a blind detective.

"You've got to have something different," they told Cannell.

As if Jim Rockford wasn't different enough already. So what did the men in the Black Tower have in mind?

"They asked, 'Have you ever seen *Electra Glide in Blue*?' " Cannell recalled.

The motion picture in question was a 1973 film starring Robert Blake as a pint-size motorcycle cop.

"In the movie, there were a lot of jokes about his being short—a short motorcycle cop " Dannell said. "And Universal was high on Robert Blake. They wanted to do something with him.

"'Make our P.I. five-foot-six,' they told us, 'and you'll have a five-year hit.' "

But Huggins and Cannell weren't convinced.

CASTING DIFFERENCES

"We felt it needed better casting than Robert Blake," Cannell said. "I mean, it wasn't like Universal was wrong about him. He was great in *Baretta*—(a show for which Cannell wrote the first script and Huggins produced). It was on for four years, you know.

"It's just we felt he wasn't the right kind of actor to play Rockford. After all, if he's small and he quits every time he gets threatened, people are going to think he's a coward."

Instead, Cannell and Huggins wanted an actor who was big enough—size-wise, that is—to look like another Mannix type. Then and only then, Cannell insisted, would it be funny whenever Rockford let his yellow streak show.

Huggins wanted James Garner.

ENTER GARNER

They had worked together on *Maverick*, the series that made Garner a star in the late '50s.

Garner had turned to TV for the first time in more than a decade in 1971 with the short-lived *Nichols*, a Western with *Maverick* touches but lacking the *Maverick* panache.

The Rockford Files, Huggins reasoned, was right up Garner's alley.

"Here's the way I remember it going down," Cannell said.

"We were trying to figure out what to do with this script, get it a better piece of casting than Robert Blake. Then Roy's thinking 'You know what we've got here is a contemporary *Maverick*. We've got to get this to James Garner.' "

Garner, in fact, was hunting for a new project at the time. He was on the verge of signing a deal at MGM.

Meta Rosenberg, Garner's managing agent and soon-to-be executive producer of *The Rockford Files*, picks up the story:

"Jim and I were looking at another script at Metro. Every studio in town wanted him—Fox, Warner Brothers, Metro, Universal. All of them were sending us scripts.

"Then Steve's script came in. We just loved it. It was the best one that we'd read by far. Steve had created a wonderful character."

A mere 72 hours later, Garner was signed to do *The Rockford Files*.

"When you read something you like as much as we liked Steve's script " Rosenberg said, "you don't waste time. You go after it."

Added Cannell: "I'm told that if we'd gotten the script to Jim just two days later, he probably would have gone ahead and signed with MGM—and it (Garner as Rockford) never would have happened."

That isn't to say, of course, it was smooth sailing from then on.

SELLING THE SERIES

After all, even though *The Rockford Files* had a star, it still didn't have a network.

The studio was reluctant to bring the 90-minute film to ABC, because the network brass had disliked the script so vehemently when proposed for *Toma*. Universal brass, in fact, feared the other networks would react the same way.

"So Frank Price (an executive at Universal) called J. J. McMann at NBC," Cannell said. "and he said, 'We've got *The Rockford Files* with James Garner. Do you want it? Yes or no.'

"McMann said it sounded interesting; when could he look at the script? And Frank Price said, 'You can't read it. You'll have to tell me now. Yes or no.'

"Well, NBC went ahead bought it—sight unseen—and when they finally read the script, they hated it too."

Too late. With its network commitment, the pilot was shot in February 1974. Swerling served as the film's executive producer and Cannell as its producer.

Though NBC wasn't particularly high on the film—Huggins said the network was "negative as hell"—*The Rockford Files* was telecast March 27, 1974, when a 90-minute slot opened and the network needed an emergency filler.

Viewer reaction was impressive enough for the network to change its tune and in April, it commissioned a series.

Jim Rockford had proven the network nay-sayers wrong.

It's a fortunate thing for us Rockford fans that he did.

CHAPTER FOUR:

A CASE OF CHEMISTRY

James Garner and Stuart Margolin.

The difference between a good show and a great one?

Chemistry!

Colorful characters, inventive plot twists and a crack production crew can carry a television series only so far, for the recipe still lacks a crucial ingredient without the right cast to pull it all together.

On the other hand, a dynamic cast can't do much with inferior material, can it?

Simply put, the mix has to be just right, which explains why bad shows outnumber immortal ones.

Consider the magic of *I Love Lucy* and *The Andy Griffith Show*, of *Star Trek* and *Perry Mason*. Chemistry, on screen and off, played a large part in making those shows classics.

The same is true for *The Rockford Files*, a series with an on-screen team that was assembled in casting heaven and behind-the- scenes players who kept everything going smoothly.

ROCKFORD'S CHEMISTRY

First, the characters:

Unlike countless other shows that weren't nearly as memorable, Rockford didn't particularly need a steady stream of offbeat guest stars to keep things lively. Instead, the moments that made this series great most often were produced internally.

With supporting cast members like Noah Beery Jr. as Rocky, (our hero's salt-of-the-earth father), Joe Santos (as Dennis Becker, the all-important police contact) and, of course, Stuart Margolin (as Angel, the sleazeball ex-con who made Rockford's sneakiness seem knightly noble by comparison), the world of Jim Rockford was topsy- turvy enough already.

Broadly drawn recurring characters like Lance White (played by Tom Selleck), Gandy Fitch (Isaac Hayes) and Rita Capkovic (Rita Moreno) made the series even zestier, to be sure. But the regular cast was what gave Rockford its week-in, week-out bankability.

As star James Garner said of the characters: "If you don't know who they are you're not going to understand too much of (the show). In a series like *The Rockford Files,* you have to watch steadily to know what's going on."

Indeed, as was the case in *I Love Lucy, Andy Griffith* and the rest, many of the sights and sounds that gave Rockford its charm were ongoing bits that somehow never seemed to get repetitive.

There was Rocky's nonstop pestering that his son take a wife, settle down and find a new, more-respectable line of work, like long-distance trucking, perhaps.

There was Becker's unmasked aggravation whenever "Jimbo" showed up at police headquarters, asking for favors and information from police files that Becker really had no business doling out.

And who can forget Angel's harebrained scams and his knack for involving "Jimmy" in them whenever they went sour?

As with those other classic series, in which popular bits were used time and again with only slight variation, familiarity on *The Rockford Files* bred anything but contempt.

Santos saw it this way: "The chemistry in the show worked very, very well—the tongue-in-cheek humor—and an outsider couldn't just come in and make the humor work. It came from the regular characters and their relationships to one another.

"It was a case of the actors learning about their characters and the writers learning about the actors. It took time developing those on-screen relationships.

"But the longer the show lasted, the more those relationships paid off."

Indeed, these ingredients—an ideal mix of fine acting, fresh writing and intuitive casting—were what made the series go.

CASTING ROCKFORD

"We hired only people we knew we could work with, both on and off camera," said Meta Rosenberg, who as executive producer did all the casting. "It was important that everyone understood what the show was all about, what its attitude would be.

"It didn't just become a good show. It was a solid show from the very beginning because we made it that way."

The first and most crucial stroke, of course, was matching Garner with the central character.

"I can't conceive of any other actor in the role," Stephen J. Cannell said. "Jim was able to pull off that tongue-in-cheek sense of humor. He played it just right, the same way he had in the *Maverick* series.

"He made Rockford his role."

Did he ever!

Viewers these days would no more accept an actor other than Garner in the role of Jim Rockford than they would someone other Raymond Burr portraying Perry Mason or Peter Falk playing Lieutenant Columbo.

Garner, quite simply, became Jim Rockford, the one and the only.

"Jim played the character in a way no one else could play him," said Rosenberg. "He's a wonderful actor."

Garner can rightfully claim only part of credit. Without the initial brush strokes from Dannell and Roy Huggins—as well as important contributions from writer/producer David Chase and Juanita Bartlett and freelance writer Gordon Dawson, to name but a few—the Rockford character couldn't have been nearly as intriguing or entertaining.

As Garner put it: "I didn't bring anything to it. I just showed up and said the words."

Of course, Garner had far more input than he liked to let on. He was, after all, a part owner in the series—his Cherokee Productions partnering with Universal Studios and Huggins' Public Arts. And Rockford's production personnel consisted largely of Garner's handpicked favorites, people with whom had previously worked and developed a rapport.

A FAMILIAR CREW

Stunt coordinator Roy Clark and stand-in Luis Delgado, for instance, first met Garner back in his *Maverick* days, as did Rockford's chief electrician, Gibby Germmine.

Cinematographer Andrew Jackson befriended Garner nearly a decade before *The Rockford Files* went into production. Film editor George Rohrs and makeup man Dick Blair were longtime Garner favorites as well. Bartlett, a writer-turned-producer, was once Rosenberg's secretary at Cherokee.

"Our people in the crew (were) handpicked," Jackson said, "not only for their ability, but for their personality."

Rosenberg, for that matter, even fell into that category. His agent since 1957, when *Maverick* debuted, she served as executive producer in each of Garner's post-*Maverick* television series.

"One of the first things I saw to was that Steve Cannell would continue to be involved in the show," Rosenberg said. "He created a wonderful character and I felt we needed him if the show was to remain as good as the pilot had been."

The strategy with which this production team was assembled paid handsomely too—as only one noteworthy behind-the-scenes battle marred an otherwise smoothly-run operation.

During the first season Huggins and Garner had a falling out involving control of the series, differences that resulted in Huggins' not being allowed to set foot on the set.

Huggins said the feud finally was patched up some years after the series ran its course—but to this day Huggins maintains it was he, in an uncredited capacity, who laid the groundwork that made Rockford a success. Rosenberg, on the other hand, was quick to contradict, stating that Huggins "was only with the show a couple of weeks."

No matter. Regardless who the boss may have been, the fact remains that both made significant contributions; that the on- screen product was sound throughout the series' stay on the air and that Garner, as Rockford, had never been better.

Equally as impressive was the ease with which Garner's supporting players fit into their roles.

ROCKY

Noah Beery, for instance, wasn't the only actor to appear as Joseph Rockford, our hero's father—but he certainly was the only one who really counted.

"We always wanted Pidge for that part," Cannell said. "What a pro.

But the timing wouldn't allow Beery, a seasoned character actor, to play Rockford's father in the movie pilot. In February 1974, when filming for the Rockford pilot took place, Beery was committed to another series, Doc Elliot, a short-lived medical drama starring James Franciscus.

Someone else would have to do.

The original Rocky, therefore, was an unheralded actor by the name of Robert Donley.

"The Rocky we used in the pilot was a good actor," Rosenberg said. "But he didn't fit the role as Jim's father quite as believably as we'd have liked. Noah Beery, on the other hand—he was perfect."

Casting in this case was anything but pure whim, mind you. After all, the Rocky character was one that was particularly close to Cannell's heart.

"From the start I wanted Rockford to have a blue-collar father, the salt of the earth," said Cannell, who saw this as another way of deviating from the conventional "loner" detective scenario.

"Here was a guy who thought his son was a real Bozo, a guy who was slightly embarrassed by what his son did for a living. Yet underneath it all you could always tell they were close. That's the way my father (who owned an interior design firm) was when I told him I wanted to be a writer.

"That's why I named the character Joseph. I named him after my father."

And, as Rocky, Beery was a marvel.

Capturing the feel of the character to the letter, he was precisely what Cannell envisioned. He was thoroughly convincing in the role.

"Noah Beery was Steve's contribution completely," Huggins recalled. "Steve always wanted him instead of the other guy. They look a little alike (Garner and Beery). Maybe that's why."

Yet Cannell and Rosenberg maintained it was strictly a case of chemistry.

"We picked him because of his warmth," said Rosenberg.

In *TV Guide* 's initial analysis of the series, critic Cleveland Amory described Beery's character as being "either a bit much or very good at making much out of his bit."

That was true in a sense, for even though Beery appeared in only a fraction of the scenes that featured Garner, he made a lasting impression nonetheless.

ANGEL

The real scene stealer—the actor who was best at "making much out of his bit"—was Stuart Margolin.

Evelyn Martin, the lowlife ex-con with the oxymoronic moniker of Angel, was a character conceived merely as a one-time role in the series pilot.

"I had this scene in which Rockford was gathering evidence, pure exposition " Cannell recalled. "It's the kind of scene that can be pretty boring. All detective shows have them.

"But there's an old trick in mystery writing: You can get past the exposition with a good piece of attitude. And that's where Angel came in."

The scene took Rockford to a newspaper morgue, where Angel, his former San Quentin cellmate, worked. Rockford asked Angel to look up some information for him.

"And in the process of Rockford getting the information he needs," Cannell said, "this whole other scene is being played out, with Angel trying to get Rockford to admit he really committed the crime he was sent to prison for."

The exchange went like this:

Angel: "If I didn't have to keep this crummy job, I'd quit. You don't know what it's like being on parole. I gotta check in once a week with some fish called Norman Carter and I got to tell him how it's going. If my brother-in-law didn't own this paper, I probably wouldn't ever got out of prison. Ho, I'm stuck, baby. Stuck."

Rockford: "Sorry to hear it, Angel."

Angel: "It's okay. I guess I had it coming. I did that bank."

Rockford: "Yeah? When we were in, you must've told me a hundred times you were innocent."

Angel: "Well, I wasn't. How about you?"

Rockford: "Huh?"

Angel: "You really do it?"

Rockford: "No, I was bad-rapped.

Angel: "Sure, sure. Look, I told you. Come on, give it to me straight. You were in that robbery, right?"

Rockford: "Wrong."

Angel: "I don't believe you."

Rockford: "Nobody ever did."

Angel: "Come on, just between us. You were dirty, right? What the hell? I won't tell."

Rockford: "No, I never pulled the job."

Angel. "Okay, you want it that way? I never did the bank either."

Angel's ultimate payoff line, meanwhile, came in his only other scene, when he told Rockford's client, "Jim and me go way back. Was in the pen together. We was both framed."

From those two richly comic scenes came one of the most colorful creeps in the history of series television.

"Angel's an absolute masterpiece," Huggins said. "Steve has a real genius for creating the offbeat character. If anyone else had written that script, there never would have been an Angel. He's Steve's invention all the way."

It was Rosenberg, however, who applied the next brush stroke by matching the character with the actor.

"I had worked with Stuart Margolin in *Nichols*," she said. "Once I read Steve's script, right away I thought of Stu. I knew he'd be right. He had played the same underhanded type of character in *Nichols*."

Added Cannell: "It was just supposed to be that one time, but he was so good we just kept bringing him back."

Good, indeed. Margolin ultimately won "best supporting actor" Emmys in 1979 and 1980, acing out fellow Rockford regulars Beery and Santos in the process.

"I was crazy about Angel," said Margolin. "What a great character. When I started playing him, I pictured him as a composite of my Nichols character and some of the street people I'd encountered while growing up in Dallas. I used to refer to Angel as an 'urban rat.'

"I was proud of the work I did on Rockford because I really achieved what I set out to do with my character."

Never mind that in six seasons Margolin appeared in just 29 episodes of *The Rockford Files*. He made a lasting impression nonetheless.

"People have often remarked to me about that," he said. "It seems they have the impression I was in a lot more shows than I actually was. I suppose it just goes to show how good the character was.

"It was such a well written role—and, of course, a lot of it was working with James Garner. We had the same feel for what was funny and what wasn't. We had good timing together."

There's that chemistry connection again.

BECKER

Joe Santos' presence, meanwhile, was in large part Cannell's doing.

"He played a Mafia hit man in the first *Toma*," Cannell recalled. "He hadn't been an actor all that long, but he was brilliant just the same.

"I remembered him when it came time to cast Becker."

Sergeant Dennis Becker—a character Cannell named after a close friend, a Los Angeles stockbroker—was more conventional than Rocky and Angel by pure necessity. After all, no matter how many ways Rockford flaunted the conventions of the TV detective, he still would need a police contact.

Nonetheless, Cannell refused to cave in completely to tradition. He made Becker not some high-ranking member of the police force, but rather an in-the-trenches sergeant.

Then Santos made his character stand out further still by modeling him after, of all people, his mother.

"She had a long-suffering, pained way about her. I used that. Whenever Jim would come in wanting some favor, I'd sigh and go, 'jeez, what am I getting into now? I'm gonna get in trouble. Aw,

to hell with it. What do you want this time?'

"Pretty soon the writers started writing the character like that, which made it a great deal easier. That was how the relationships developed over the years; a little touch here, a little touch there.

"It's like the 'Jimbo' thing. That wasn't in the script either. It just came out of the clear blue one day. I called him Jimbo. It fit. After that I called him Jimbo all the time."

BETH

Perhaps the "straightest" regular character, meanwhile, was Beth Davenport, Rockford's attorney.

Played by Gretchen Corbett, a Shakespearean stage performer who was under contract to Universal when the series began production, Beth was the one character that wasn't in the least bit unusual.

She was a professional, a dedicated officer of the courts who, judging how often Rockford's cases landed him in jail, had a recurring role more from necessity than for color.

After all, somebody had to post his bail.

Thus, while Angel was busy stealing the spotlight with his shameless absence of conscience—one of his "finest" moments had him roping our hero into his troubles and then, when riled mobsters moved on Rockford, Angel insisted, "I'm not with him!"—Beth was stuck with perfunctory lawyer lines like, "If that's all you have, Lieutenant, then I'm leaving and I'm taking my client with me."

Ho-hum.

And not only was her role less colorful. The story of how Corbett was chosen is rather bland as well.

"We read a lot of actresses," Rosenberg said, "and she was the one we liked best. That's really all there was to it."

If anything, in fact, the passage of time has faded her uniqueness even more, for when Rockford first hit the airwaves, pretty lady lawyers weren't quite as commonplace as they are today.

That isn't to say, however, that there was no chemistry between Beth and Rockford. Little hints that at one time they had more than just a lawyer-client relationship, for instance, were plentiful.

Basically, as Beery had, Corbett made the most out of a little bit.

FUN

When guest stars like Isaac Hayes or Tom Selleck made sparks fly, meanwhile, Rosenberg, Cannell and company were quick to bring them back for more.

That was yet another approach that made *The Rockford Files* so consistently fun to watch.

As Santos put it: "We had great writers and great producers. They're the ones who gave us good characters and the good stories. And on top of that the cast was so good.

"We got to be like family—the writers, the producers, the actors. We were all very, very close and I think that's reflected in the quality of the show.

"Now I'm not saying that every show was a gem. But with the kind of love we all put into it, it's no wonder we usually had pretty good ones."

So, in the final analysis, which was more important to the success of *The Rockford Files*—the writing, the casting or the acting?

Consider that *The Rockford Files'* three-pronged variation of the age-old chicken-or-the-egg conundrum.

One really wouldn't have mattered without the others.

Mariette Hartley and James Garner move their on-screen ROCKFORD chemistry into a Polaroid commercial.

CHAPTER FIVE:

SIX YEARS OF STEADINESS

Suppose a technician at a television station attempted to move six year's worth of tapes of *The Rockford Files*, quite an armful indeed. Suppose he tripped and fell, the tapes spilling all across the floor. And suppose our hypothetical technician couldn't read a lick, meaning when he re-shelved his Rockford tapes, they'd no longer be arranged in their proper order.

Suppose all that happened and, because of it, the shows weren't telecast in their usual sequence.

So what?

With the exception of the few episodes in which recurring guest characters returned for second and third go-rounds—with storylines built around the characters' previous appearances—it really wouldn't make a bit of difference.

For unlike many long-lasting series that evolved stylistically or underwent major cast changes as the years passed, Jim Rockford and *The Rockford Files* were the picture of steadiness from beginning to end.

ROCK STEADY

Rockford didn't change much over the years. Maybe he softened his hard-line, never-take-a-case-for-free attitude a bit and certainly he became less of a rough-and-tumble customer as he continued to age. But basically Rockford didn't change. When *The Rockford Files* went off the air in 1980, our hero was still the same hard-luck, gun-shy, sneaky-clever private detective we met and fell for six years earlier.

The same is true for the show itself. No cast changes. (Gretchen Corbett left the show after four years but her character wasn't replaced.) No tinkering with its patented blend of action and humor.

"There were never really any attempts to fiddle around with the show," said Meta Rosenberg. "We knew we had something that worked and was good and we stayed with it."

SURPRISING STRENGTH

Indeed, in its first year (1974-75), *The Rockford Files* was perhaps the surprise of the season. Though not expected to fare exceptionally well—*TV Guide* handicappers, for instance, had given the show 7-2 odds of surviving the season—Rockford placed a rock-solid No. 12 in the Nielsen numbers, NBC's third-best ratings grabber.

It was the second-highest-rated detective cop series on television (after CBS's *Hawaii Five-O*, which was No. 10). And thanks to *Sanford and Son* (No. 2 in the Nielsens), *Chico and the Man* (No. 3) and Rockford, NBC literally owned Friday nights.

So why fix what wasn't broken?

The movie pilot had established all the Rockford ground rules and the debut season's episodes merely proved that the formula worked.

In *The Kirkoff Case*, the first episode, our hero took on a $20,000 case but ultimately wound up with nothing.

In *Exit Prentiss Carr*, Rockford's involvement in an active police case brought harassment from bad guys but even more heat from the cops.

In *The Big Ripoff*, he solved a major insurance swindle, but ended up collecting nothing while the bad guy arrived at a lucrative settlement with the cheated firm.

In *This Case Is Closed* and *Find Me If You Can*, he found himself being pushed around by mobsters—and not entirely certain why—because his clients hadn't been completely honest when they hired him.

And in *Profit and Loss* and *Counter Gambit*, he even resorted to a little lawbreaking and con-man trickery to solve his cases.

As the Nielsen ratings attested, Rockford and his unconventional way of doing things were just what the viewing public wanted.

CONVINCING THE BRASS

The network brass, however, wasn't convinced.

During the summer before Rockford's second season, for instance, CBS schemed to cut into the show's numbers by programming a heavy hitter, *Hawaii Five-O*, opposite it.

The move brought on panic at NBC. Network executives tried to make Rosenberg and Stephen Cannell "cut the comedy."

"They really were pressuring us," Rosenberg recalled. "NBC was afraid of the competition. Here we were, a humorous show, and *Hawaii Five-O* had no humor at all. They felt we wouldn't do well against it."

The triumvirate behind Jim Rockford refused to budge. James Garner, Rosenberg and Cannell all threatened to quit if any such changes were imposed on them.

Garner, in fact, got the point across by staging a sit-in in his dressing room until the network brass showed up to talk. He then forced them to back off by explaining that if they wanted Rockford to be like Five-O they'd have to "hire Jack Lord's younger brother" to play the lead.

Had the threesome not stood its ground, the soul very likely could have been cut out of the series.

"If you took out the humor," said Rosenberg, "the show would have ceased to exist. There simply would have been no point to it."

HOLDING HIS OWN

The results of the head-to-head Rockford-Five-O war, meanwhile, proved Rosenberg right.

True, Five-O did cut significantly into *The Rockford Files'* ratings, but it was McGarrett & Co. that tumbled the farthest. Both disappeared from the Nielsen top 25—yet it was Jim Rockford who consistently won the time slot.

"We did so well against *Hawaii Five-O*," said Rosenberg, "CBS wound up moving it away from us."

The competition that NBC brass had feared so much lasted a mere three months.

Even though *The Rockford Files* never regained its lofty first-year ratings, it performed solidly enough to enjoy a six-year stay in prime time, ending production only when Garner decided to call it quits.

In short, the Rockford team kept its legion of loyal viewers because it didn't alienate them with a lot of unnecessary tinkering. If anything, in fact, Rockford did the opposite in its second season, striving to get even more mileage from elements that had worked the first season.

BUILDING FROM STRENGTH

Stuart Margolin's Angel Martin, a real scene stealer in the movie pilot and in his three appearances during the first year, became a more prominently involved character—often there to lend a hand when Rockford worked his own con games (*The Farnsworth Strategem* and *Joey Blue Eyes*) but also there to bring plenty of trouble Rockford's way in *Chicken Little's A Little Chicken*).

The relationship between Rockford and Joe Santos' Dennis Becker developed into an abiding friendship in *The Farnsworth Strategem* and an engaging new relationship—with ex-con Sandy Fitch, the guy known in prison as "The Hammer of C Block"—was forged.

Meanwhile, Rockford continued to play the loser, suckered by friends and clients in *The Aaron Ironwood School of Success, The Real Easy Red Dog*, and *The Girl in the Bay City Boy's Club* and even more often simply in the wrong place at the wrong time (*The Great Blue Lake and Development Company, Pastoria Prime Pick* and *The No-Cut Contract*).

"That was the whole point of the show," Rosenberg said, "the fact that Rockford could get into all sorts of trouble through no fault of his own. He simply had bad luck. Trouble had a way of finding him."

Did it ever!

As the show progressed into its third and fourth seasons, that same formula continued to work like a charm.

In *The Oracle Wore A Cashmere Suit*, the episode that introduced James Luisi's blustery Lieutenant Chapman, Rockford found himself in hot water with the police merely because a less-than-reputable psychic claimed our hero was involved in a kidnapping.

In *Drought at Indianhead River*, Angel got himself—and Rockford—caught in the middle of a mob-run real-estate scam. And no sooner did Rockford bail them out than Angel was waist-deep in trouble again in *Rattlers' Class of 'BS*.

In *There's One in Every Port*, Rockford was the sap in a father-daughter con-artist team's swindle—but he settled the score with a con of his own.

In *Beamer's Last Case*, the first episode of the fourth season, Rockford returned from a vacation to discover someone had assumed his identity in his absence, wrecked Rockford's credit with a slew of charge-it purchases and badly botched a case.

In *The Queen of Peru*, tourists made off with Rockford's barbecue grill—and the multi-million-dollar diamond that had been stashed there.

And in *South by Southwest*, a spin of sorts off Alfred Hitchcock's *North by Northwest*, a case of mistaken identities got Rockford involved in a south-of-the-border espionage caper.

A LITTLE RESPECT

Indeed, Rockford might have become the poster child for hard-luck cases, but finally the show was getting the respect it deserved.

After striking out its first two seasons in the Emmy department, Garner collected "best actor" honors in 1977 and the production team of Rosenberg, Cannell, David Chase and Charles Floyd Johnson copped "best series" Emmys the following year. (Rita Moreno, meanwhile, won an Emmy in a guest appearance.)

For its fifth and sixth seasons, Margolin would reign in the "best supporting actor" category, coming a long way indeed considering his character's modest beginnings with the show.

GOOFY GUESTS

Meanwhile, more and more goofy guest stars were introduced in what became recurring roles: Rita Capkovic (Rita Moreno), Richie Brockelman (Dennis Dugan), John Cooper (Bo Hopkins), Fred Beamer (James Whitmore Jr.) and the incomparable Lance White (Tom Selleck).

And in *Paradise Cove*, the first episode of the final season, we got perhaps the best in-joke of them all: Garner and his co-star in a series of Polaroid commercials, Mariette Hartley, finally appeared together in something that lasted longer than 30 seconds.

Garner and his *Rockford Files* associates went into the 1979-80 season, meanwhile, with the full knowledge it would be their last.

END OF THE LINE

The work had taken its toll on the 52-year-old Garner, who had long since completed his original four-year commitment to play Jim Rockford. Now he was eager to call it quits.

"I didn't want to do Rockford this year," he said in the summer of 1979. "And next season definitely will be the last. It's a killer. We shoot 10 pages (of script) a day and I'm in every shot. Yeah, this will be the last."

Knowing they were winding to a close, then, a number of episodes during the final year tied up some loose ends.

In *Love Is the Word*, Rockford's romance with a beautiful blind psychologist, Megan Dougherty, was wrapped up in heartbreaking fashion—he lost the girl.

In *The No-Fault Affair*, Rita made an important career change—no longer would she be walking the streets.

And in the hilarious *Nice Guys Finish Dead*, Fred Beamer (the troublemaker from *Beamer's Last Case*) finally got his detective's license and Mr. Perfect Lance White continued his charmed existence—he married a beautiful heiress.

Then an unforeseen development forced production to screech to an abrupt halt: Garner had been hospitalized.

Among the ailments that put him in the Scripps Medical Clinic in La Jolla, Calif., were a stomach virus, numerous ulcers and sinusitis (inflammation of the sinuses).

"Jim was in very bad shape," Rosenberg said. "It was a very, very demanding role—a physical role—and he had been doing it for six years. It was 14 hours a day, six days a week—four of them of location—and Jim was in practically every shot. He was physically worn out and psychologically drained.

"The network didn't want us to quit, but when Jim checked into the Scripps Clinic it was pretty obvious how sick he was."

The series shut down production at the end of November 1979, a mere 10 episodes in the can. The final one, *Deadlock in Parma*, aired Jan. I4, 1980.

And that was the end of *The Rockford Files*—not because the series had run out of steam, but because its star had simply run out of gas.

CHAPTER SIX

THE GARNER FILE

James Garner as NICHOLS

"We're actors. We ply our trade wherever we do it. That is what we sell. We're the court jesters. That's our function—to entertain people.

"It's a hell of a lot better than laying carpet."

So said James Garner, a man who, like the characters he's best known for portraying, refuses to take himself too seriously.

JAMES SCOTT BUMGARNER

He knows whereof he speaks, too. For the story of James Scott Bumgarner is literally a rags-to-riches tale—one that reinforces the notion that making a success of oneself requires a tenuous mix of talent and luck.

James Garner had an abundance of both.

"I never really wanted to be an actor," he said. "I just wanted to have been born rich. I was 'anti' acting 'till I was 26. I did read fan magazines, though, and decided that anyone who did what they said those people did must be some kind of nut.

"I went to acting school once. I attended about seven classes and quit. It wasn't for me. Many people, of course, go into acting by design and get training.

"I know actors who are an awful lot better than I am who have not had the success I've had. But where do you place the blame for that? Fans are fickle."

There's another, more telling explanation: Like Roy Hobbs, Garner was a natural.

BIRTH OF A MAVERICK

Born April 7, 1928, in Norman, Okla., Garner was the youngest of Weldon and Mildred Bumgarner's three sons. His heritage was part German, part Cherokee. Garner's maternal grandfather was a full-blooded Cherokee Indian.

He was known as Butch Bumgarner—or "Little Bum"—throughout his childhood years and wouldn't drop the first syllable of his last name until years later, a change that coincided with his beginning an acting career.

His father was a carpet layer. His mother died when he was 5. "I remember only the funeral," he said of her.

Garner's early years was a life of poverty. When his father remarried, young Garner had to go to work.

"I had to help out. I started when I was 8 or 9, mowing lawns, 15 cents here, 20 cents there. My stepmother took most of it. It was a tough period—but I'm independent because of it."

He worked as a janitor at the University of Oklahoma at age 13, Just one of many jobs he held throughout his teenage years.

"I worked from 3:3O a.m. to 7:3O a.m. and then went to school," he said. "That was one of the low moments. God, I worked. The oil fields of Texas when I was 16, clearing trees for Bell Telephone when I was 17.

"Nothing was too tough. I worked harder than anybody."

He lettered in football, basketball and track in high school but in 1944, at age 16, he dropped out to join the Merchant Marine.

He served only briefly, then moved on to a variety of odd jobs. He was a gas station attendant, a lifeguard, a traveling salesman, a model of swimming trunks.

He even laid carpet for a time with his father, who had relocated to Los Angeles.

Garner attended the University of Oklahoma in 1947, a member of the Sooners' football program, but dropped out after injuring his knees and back.

His back injury was non-football related. It occurred while on a double date with a couple of University of Utah coeds when their car flipped in an accident.

More odd jobs followed.

Garner served in the Army's 24th Division in Korea in 1951, the first man drafted from the state of Oklahoma. During his tour of duty, in April of that year, he found himself so far behind enemy lines he was wounded by friendly fire, shot "in the backside" and burned by phosphorous artillery shells.

He would receive two Purple Hearts 32 years later, on Jan. 24, 1983, his medals delayed because of a military mix-up. "It's better to receive this now than posthumously," he said at the ceremony.

Leaving the service, it was back to work.

Garner once calculated that before becoming an actor, he held as many as 50 jobs and, "I never found one I liked."

ON THE RIGHT TRACK

One of those jobs, however, when he worked at a Hollywood gas station at age 17, would prove to be quite valuable in his launching an acting career. For it was while pumping gas that he developed a friendship with Paul Gregory, who would go on to become a successful theatrical producer.

Eight years after striking up their friendship, in 1953, Garner happened to be in Los Angeles, driving by Gregory's firm, Paul Gregory and Associates. An impulse hit him. He stopped in to see if Gregory had been serious years earlier when he told him he should become an actor.

"He owned the building," Garner said. "There was a parking space there so I just pulled in. If that space hadn't been there, I would never have driven around the block to look for one."

The visit paid off. Gregory gave Garner a job cuing Lloyd Nolan during rehearsals of his Broadway production of *The Caine Mutiny Court Martial* and in time he would work his way up to his first acting role, a non-speaking part in which he sat on stage for two hours as one of six jurors.

FIRST ROLES

Garner gave 512 performances without uttering so much as a syllable, but it proved to be a valuable learning experience.

"I watched Henry (Fonda) every night," he said, "and I swiped practically all my acting from him. I just listened."

Shortly after *The Caine Mutiny Court Martial* came Garner's first television appearance—a commercial. In it, he made famous the much-berated phrase, "Winston tastes good like a cigarette should."

"That's the way I did it," he said, "and a year later they did a whole ad campaign to cross 'like' out and put 'as' in its place."

To this day he is unsure whether the line was grammatically incorrect in the script or if he merely read it wrong.

That was hardly the end of Garner's career as a TV pitchman, however. Years later he and actress Mariette Hartley would be featured in a popular series of commercials for Polaroid. In those ads, the two were so convincing at friendly husband/wife bickering many viewers mistakenly believed they were married. Hartley even took to wearing a T-shirt that read, "James Garner is not my husband."

Garner's real wife was former actress Lois Clarke, to whom he was married in 1957. They raised two daughters; one became an elementary school teacher, the other a Nashville country singer.

MAVERICK

As for Garner's post-Winston acting career, it was about to skyrocket. Warner Brothers signed him to a contract in 1956 and *Maverick*, the series that brought him celebrity, was just around the corner.

He made his motion picture debut in *Toward the Unknown*, a 1956 film directed by Mervyn LeRoy and starring William Holden and Lloyd Nolan. Other pre-Maverick film credits included *The Girl He Left Behind* (1956), *Shoot Out at Medicine Bend* (1957) and *Sayonara* (1957). He also appeared in such TV series as *Cheyenne* and *Conflict*, both of which were produced by Roy Huggins.

Then, in 1957, Huggins and *Maverick* made Garner a star.

"I was doing *Sayonara* when Warner Brothers was looking at every actor in Hollywood for *Maverick*. Then they noticed me in the dailies and said, 'Let's use him. He's already under contract.' I did the pilot and when I got back from Japan I started *Maverick*."

The tongue-in-cheek anti-Western was a phenomenal success, holding down one of the spots in the Nielsen ratings by its second season, and Garner's presence was indisputably the element that made it work.

His "overnight" success, in turn, led to more and better motion picture roles. But the next major development in his acting career involved a real-life drama, Garner's part in an on-again, off-again war that was brewing with television's powers that be.

The battle was over money.

In the beginning Warner Brothers was paying Garner $500 a week—not bad for a beginning actor—yet his seven-year contract with the studio was a rather oppressive one. It didn't allow any outside money-making enterprises, such as personal appearances, and he received no residuals.

"My competition was Ed Sullivan, who got $25,000 a week."

Even though his salary jumped to $800 a week during the second year of Maverick and $1,250 a week his third, Garner saw it as a pittance compared to the millions Warners was raking in from the hit series.

So in 1960, after a writers' strike briefly crippled the studio, Garner took advantage of a loophole in his contract: Warner Brothers had suspended him for two months, supposedly as punishment for his involvement with the writers union, and Garner countered by suing the studio for breach of contract.

The battle with the studio was reminiscent of one that *Cheyenne*'s Clint Walker had two years earlier, in which the star walked out because of a money dispute. But unlike Walker, who ultimately buckled and returned to the Warner Brothers fold, a court sided with Garner, declaring him free from his contract in December 1960.

Maverick would carry on for another two seasons without Garner—aside from his appearances in repeat episodes, from which the network got plenty of mileage—yet the series could never recapture the magic or the ratings of its early years.

FILMS

As for Garner's film career, meanwhile, during his *Maverick* years he had appeared in *Darby's Rangers* (1958), a World War II film that represented his first starring role in a motion picture, and *Up Periscope* (1959).

But now emancipated from Warners, he could launch a motion picture career in earnest.

Over the next 15 years he would star in more than two dozen films—some good, some critically acclaimed, others not so good or well-received.

The first was *Cash McCall* (1960). Bigger ones quickly followed.

Among the highlights: *The Children's Hour* (1962), *The Great Escape* (1963), *The Americanization of Emily* (1964) and *Duel at* Diablo (1966).

His talent for light comedy, meanwhile, led to roles in such films as *Boys' Night Out* (1962), *The Thrill of It All* (1963), *Move Over, Darling* (1963), *The Art of Love* (1965), *Support Your Local Sheriff* (1971) and *Skin Game* (1972).

Of those credits, *The Americanization of Emily*, a widely praised film in which he co-starred with Julie Andrews, Melvyn Douglas and James Coburn, is said to be his favorite.

Television had become just a bad memory. Once asked about the potential of his ever working in TV again, Garner reportedly responded: "TV? What's that?"

His self-imposed exile from TV would not last. A dwindling selection of quality film roles and the lure of a $1 million-a-year contract were factors in his change of heart.

BACK TO TV

With his own company, Cherokee Productions (so named in tribute to his grandfather), partnering with Universal Studios, Garner starred in *Nichols*, an offbeat Western series. Garner played the title character.

The series, and his character, combined elements of *Maverick* with *Support Your Local Sheriff*. *Nichols*—a scheming, somewhat cowardly man with no known first name—had become the unwilling sheriff of a 1914 Arizona town. The most memorable moment the series had to offer though, came in the final episode, in which Nichols was gunned down and killed, only to be avenged by his heroic brother, Jim Nichols (also played by Garner).

Though the series was a ratings disaster and lasted only one season, it is said to have been Garner's favorite series.

Two years later, however, the television success Garner had been hoping for finally came. It was as private investigator Jim Rockford in *The Rockford Files*.

In 1974 *Time* magazine heralded his presence as "the most welcome return" to television.

In 1977 he won an Emmy for "outstanding lead in a drama series." (He was nominated three other times during Rockford's stay on the air.

It was a role he would play for six years, until production of the series ended midway through the 1979-80 season.

NBC begrudgingly canceled the series when, at the end of November 1979, Garner was hospitalized, unable to report for filming at Universal Studios. Garner already had said it would be his last season as Rockford, but now he claimed he was too sick to finish the season, citing a variety of ailments—a stomach virus, ulcers, sinusitis and arthritic knees.

Indeed, an ailing back and bad knees had plagued him ever since his football days. "I was a physical mess," he said. "I had three operations on my knee (during the first five years Rockford). It's shot. I broke a finger, some ribs, a bone in my spine. I have broken some knuckles. You just get tired."

He also had four compressed disks in his spine.

Universal Studios executives, however, indicated a suspicion that Garner simply had tired of the role and was using his ailments as a convenient way out. It was perhaps the first volley to be heard in a new battle between Garner and a major studio.

For though Garner returned to NBC a year later, reprising his first major TV role in *Bret Maverick*, his scheming-but-lovable character now settled down in an unsuspecting little town called Sweetwater, Garner's differences with Universal and its parent company, MCA, soon took a far uglier turn.

LAWSUITS

In the March 1981 issue of *Playboy,* he accused the studio of cheating him out of millions of dollars in profits. In July 1983 he sued Universal for $22.5 million, alleging he was gypped out of profits he was entitled to from *The Rockford Files* reruns and foreign sales.

"I feel like I'm in a business with the biggest bunch of crooks you could ever get together," he was quoted as saying, "The Mafia's not as big as these people."

Figures reported by *Barron's* seemed to support his claim: As of 1989 syndication and foreign sales had amounted to $126 million. But Garner, who was entitled to a percentage, received a mere $670,000. The studio claimed the rest was eaten up by expenses.

"I always felt Rockford was my annuity," he said. "And I'll be damned if I'm going to have somebody take it away from me."

Nearly six years later, in the spring of 1989, Garner and Universal reached an out-of-court settlement.

One of the contingencies of the settlement was that neither party would discuss details of the arrangement—yet Garner came out "a big winner." The settlement reportedly called for Universal to pay Garner a whopping $10 million.

"About everything I ever have done, in the way of lawsuits against studios, I've won them all," he said. "Because I was right every time."

EXPANDING HIS ROLES

Since his last stab at series television with *Bret Maverick,* meanwhile, Garner's interest has turned to a wider variety of roles, including a number of character roles, the kind Melvyn Douglas and Wallace Beery did in their 5Os and 6Os.

"I've got no business doing that macho leading-man crap (any more)," he said. "I'm too old for it, physically too beat and mentally too beat. I'm at the point where people are not going to believe that macho hero type."

His subsequent film and television credits, accordingly, have varied widely in style, quality and acclaim.

He starred in such films as *The Fan* (1981), with Lauren Bacall; *Victor/Victoria* (1982), opposite Julie Andrews; *Tank* (1984), with C. Thomas Howell: *Murphy's Romance* (1985), opposite Sally Fields and *Sunset* (1988), alongside Bruce Willis. He was nominated for an Academy Award for his performance in *Murphy's Romance*, his only such honor despite appearing in more than 30 films.

He starred in *The Long Summer of George Adams,* a 1982 made-for-TV movie directed by Stuart Margolin; co-starred with Mary Tyler Moore in *Heartsounds,* a 1984 made-for-TV movie that marks the only film in which Garner's character dies during the course of the story; and teamed up again with Margolin in *The Glitter Dome,* a 1984 made-for-cable movie.

Garner also starred as Norman Grant, a World War II hero-turned- U.S. senator, in *Space,* a five-part, 13-hour miniseries telecast by CBS in April 1985. When *Space* aired. Garner was pictured on the cover of *People* magazine, which proclaimed him "The Last Real Man."

Garner's Cherokee Productions, which he oversees with partner Peter Duchow, has produced a number of acclaimed television movies. The first was *Promise,* a 1986 effort starring Garner and James Woods.

In *Promise* Garner played a bachelor whose lifestyle changes after the death of his mother, as he must honor a promise he made to care for his schizophrenic brother. The film won five Emmys.

Then came *My Name Is Bill.* The 1989 effort again co-starred Woods and chronicled the early days of the Alcoholics Anonymous program.

In 1990, in *Decoration Day,* Garner starred as a retired judge asked to champion the cause of a black World War II veteran who has refused to accept a U.S. government medal of honor for bravery.

"Each one has its merits," Garner said. "*Promise* dealt with a subject that was never dealt with before, schizophrenia. It might have been dealt with, but not the way we did. And Bill W. was the Alcoholics Anonymous story, which nobody has ever done before. And here's another story (*Decoration Day*) that deals with people."

HEARTSOUNDS

Of his work over the past decade, Garner has singled out *Heartsounds*. He says the unlikely Norman Lear production in which he played a doctor felled by a series of debilitating heart attacks was a significant turning point in his career.

"When *Heartsounds* came along and Norman Lear thought I could do it, I was very pleased with that."

Garner played Harold Lear, Norman's real-life cousin, in what is often regarded as his best, most compelling performance. He was so convincing in his portrayal of a sick, dying man, in fact, he said friends expressed concern about his health in real life after having seen the film.

"Most of the things I've done since Rockford have been that sort of thing," he said. "For me, no more car chases. I'm interested only in stories emphasizing human relationships."

NO MORE CAR CHASES

Garner's various ailments, meanwhile, have continued to plague him over the years. The biggest scare came in March 1988 when he was hospitalized because of a weakness in the aorta, the main artery carrying blood from the heart.

He underwent a bypass operation and surgery on the aorta.

Since that scare he has learned to slow down. "(The operation) made me smell the roses a little more, I guess," he said. "Partial retirement is great. You ought to be able to enjoy your life."

That being the case, he said, another series is highly unlikely. "People have no idea how hard an hour-long series is. Even if I did a half-hour show I'd have to work hard, especially to maintain the integrity of it.

"I'm just not working as hard as I used to. I'm getting more picky."

As of late 1990, incidentally, he was on the verge of selling his home in the Brentwood section of Los Angeles, hoping to buy a 26-acre wine-country plot in California's Santa Ynez Valley, where he planned to build his new home.

And after four decades in the acting business, Garner still refuses to take himself or his craft too seriously.

"I'm not the best actor in the world," he said, "but I think I do pretty well."

Indeed, an understatement if ever there was one.

James Garner in
UP PERISCOPE

CHAPTER SEVEN:

THE CANNELL FILE

His work represents a fine mix of quality and quantity, a combination that's quite uncommon in television today.

Then again, that's Stephen Joseph Cannell, a man whose ability is anything but common.

Over the past two decades, Cannell has closely involved himself in the writing, production and direction of more than two dozen television series. He has created or co-created more than 20 shows (more than anyone in the history of television), written more than 200 episodes of the series he created and produced or executive produced more than 500 episodes.

Indeed, since his involvement in *The Rockford Files*, the series that put him on the map, he has become a giant in the television industry. He may be the most widely known producer of cop/detective shows this side of Jack Webb and Quinn Martin.

Webb, the man who brought us *Dragnet*, was so well known because he was his own biggest star. Martin's name, meanwhile, was burned into our memories because every series he produced hammered home that fact—with an announcer who, after naming a particular series during the opening credits, followed up with the words, "a Quinn Martin production."

SIGNATURE SERIES

The signature that identifies Cannell's work, on the other hand, has more to do with content. His shows, the bulk of them of the cop/detective variety, are fresh, funny, action-packed and always full of surprises. Only the Richard Levinson-William Link team that brought us *Columbo* and Steven Bochco, of *Hill Street Blues/L.A. Law* fame, belong in the same league.

Longtime associate Roy Huggins describes Cannell as having "a real genius for creating the offbeat character." But that's only part of it.

Cannell's true genius is an ability to give us programming that works on two levels. His shows are rousing adventures that conform to long-established traditions of television. At the same time, they poke a few holes in the balloon.

"I like to have fun with it," Cannell said. "I like to take chances."

That he has.

Aside from Rockford, some of his most successful and offbeat series include *The A-Team*, *Hunter*, *Wiseguy*, *21 Jump Street*, *Riptide* and *The Greatest American Hero*.

INSIDE JOKE

Cannell's playful spirit was never more apparent, however, than his recurring inside joke in *Tenspeed and Brown Shoe*, a 1980 buddy-detective series starring Ben Vereen and Jeff Goldblum. In it, Goldblum's character, Lionel "Brown Shoe" Whitney, was a straight-laced square peg who yearned to be a hard-boiled sleuth, the kind of rough-and-tumble customer he so admired in a series of seamy sex-and-violence pulp novels penned by—get this—Stephen J. Cannell.

COMING UP THE HARD WAY

He's one of television's most colorful and prolific writers. Yet throughout his childhood years, learning to read proved to be a real battle.

Born Feb. 5, 1941, in Pasadena, a third-generation Californian, Cannell struggled in his early years, flunking out of two schools and having to repeat grades three times. It turned out he was dyslexic.

Because he experienced the hardships that parents and teachers may force on dyslexic children, he has become a spokesperson on the subject and serves as National Chairperson for the Orton Dyslexia Society. He even sponsored and performed in *Gifts of Greatness*, a filmed play depicting famous dyslexics in history, the video of which is used as an educational tool in many schools.

"I was a classic case," he said, "a real slow learner. It took a lot of understanding and therapy to overcome my problems."

But overcome those problems he did.

Cannell's desire to write for television developed during his teens. After graduation from the University of Oregon, he began to work in his father's interior design firm, Cannell and Chafin, leaving each afternoon at 5 to write on his own until 10 p.m.

FIRST BREAK

His first break came selling *Mission: Impossible* script ideas to Desilu, although he was considered too young and inexperienced to write the actual scripts. Cannell kept at it for the next four years, honing his skills with his after-hours script writing, before he was able to make his next sale, a script for an episode *It Takes a Thief*.

Encouraged by that success, he left the field of interior design for good.

In 1970 Cannell submitted a script to Universal Studios for the Jack Webb series, *Adam 12*. The producers and actors were so impressed by the story and dialogue that Cannell was immediately asked to serve as head writer.

While working at Universal, he gained the respect of his colleagues for his skills as a writer and his instincts as a creator of new shows. By the 1973-74 season he was an established talent. He was involved in two shows that year, as the creator of *Chase*, another of Webb's Mark VII productions, and as the producer and top writer of *Toma*, a series that carried Huggins' public Arts banner.

It was Cannell's involvement in *Toma*, in fact, that led to *The Rockford Files*. The 1974 pilot movie for the James Garner vehicle came directly from a discarded *Toma* script he had written.

When *Toma* ended production after one season, not because it was canceled but because leading man Tony Musante had tired of series television, Cannell shifted his attention to *The Rockford Files*. He served for the next six seasons in the capacity of supervising producer.

THE ROCKFORD FILES

Cannell's involvement in *The Rockford Files* was no small thing. He closely oversaw the writing—authoring many of the more memorable episodes himself—but also involved himself in all major aspects of production. He even directed a handful of episodes.

In fact. he owns the distinction of having been involved with *The Rockford Files* longer that any other individual, including Garner, spanning from the creation of the Rockford character to the series' last episode.

And though Rockford kept him busy, Cannell still managed to find the time for other projects:

He was the creator of *Baretta* (1975-78), a cop show starring Robert Blake; co-creator of *City of Angels* (1976), a '20s detective series starring Wayne Rogers; creator and executive producer of *Baa Baa Black Sheep* (1976-78), a World War II aviation drama starring Robert Conrad and a handful of recurring Rockford players (Simon Oakland, James Whitmore Jr. and W.K. Stratton); co-creator and executive producer of *Richie Brockelman, P.I.*, (1978), a detective series featuring a character from two Rockford episodes: creator and executive producer of *The Duke* (1979), starring Conrad as a former boxer-turned-private detective: and creator and executive producer of *Stone* (1980), starring Dennis Weaver as a homicide detective/crime novelist.

Aside from *Baretta*, with which Cannell had no ties after writing the series pilot, none of those shows lasted particularly long—*Brockelman*, in fact, a mere five episodes; *The Duke* only four. Cannell was on the verge of greatness nonetheless.

Since the swan song of *The Rockford Files* during the 1979-80 season, nary a season has passed without at least one Cannell production on the air.

HIS OWN COMPANY

In 1979 Cannell decided to form his own independent production company, Stephen J. Cannell Productions Inc., in order to achieve and maintain "creative control." The company started off with *Tenspeed and Brown Shoe* in January 1980.

In 1986, a parent company, The Cannell Studios, was formed to oversee all aspects of the company's operations.

The Cannell Studios, which has become the largest independent supplier of prime-time television, has surpassed the $800 million production mark and has experienced remarkable growth in areas such as comedy, commercials, merchandising, motion pictures and miniseries, as well as first-

run, off-network programming. The company has one of the highest percentage records of pilots that have gone to series.

The company's North Shore Studios, meanwhile, houses Cannell Films of Canada and is Canada's largest full-service production facility.

Despite his success in the production field, however, Cannell considers himself first and foremost a writer.

"This is the only studio in town that I know of that's run by a writer for writers," he said. "If I ever stopped producing or running a studio, I'd still be writing.

"I spend too much time at a typewriter to be called anything but a writer."

Among Cannell's most notable credits since forming his own company:

The Greatest American Hero (1981-83), a tongue-in-cheek parody of superhero shows with William Katt in the title role.

The A-Team (1983-87), a madcap, almost cartoonish action/adventure series that starred George Peppard, Mr. T, Dirk Benedict and Dwight Schultz and was a ratings bonanza, ranking No. 10 in the Nielsens for the 1982-83 season, No. 4 in 1983-84 and No. 6 in 1984-85.

Hardcastle and McCormick (1983-86), a buddy-detective series matching a crusty ex-judge (played by Brian Keith) and an ex-con (Daniel Hugh-Kelly), ranking No. 25 its first season.

Riptide (1984-86), another buddy-detective series, starring Perry King and Joe Penny, that rated No. 18 for the 1983-84 season and No. 14 the year after.

Hunter, a cop show starring ex-football star Fred Dryer as TV's answer to Dirty Harry. (The series debuted in 1984 and though its ratings were never exactly eye-popping its endurance has been. The series started its seventh season in 1990.)

21 Jump Street, a teen-oriented cop show that marked one of the Fox network's first programs in 1987.

Wiseguy, a cult favorite starring Ken Wahl as an undercover federal agent, a series that never has commanded high ratings but has been widely acclaimed nonetheless.

Other Cannell productions include *The Quest* (1982), *The Rousters* (1983), *The Last Precinct* (1986), *Stingray* (1986-87), *J. J. Starbuck* (1987-

88), *Sonny Spoon* (1987), *Top of the Hill* (1989) and *Booker* (1989).

Aside from his 1978 Emmy for *The Rockford Files*, Cannell has won two Edgars from the Mystery Writers of America (for *Toma* and *Stone*); a Writers Guild Award (for *Tenspeed and Brown Shoe*); the International Film and Television Award (for *The Greatest American Hero*); and four Media Access Awards (two for *Wiseguy*, one for *Hunter* and one as "Outstanding Media Employer").

He also has received three other Emmy nominations, seven Writers Guild nominations and two People's Choice nominations.

PICKING A FAVORITE

There's one disadvantage, however, to having all these screen credits jammed into one resume:

Cannell finds it extremely difficult to pick a favorite.

"I can't really single out a favorite because I love something about all of them," he said. "I loved Rockford. It was a really special show and we had such good people. In six years Jim Garner never gave me a moment's grief.

"I loved *The Greatest American Hero*. It was a lot of fun to do. And I loved *The A-Team*, the first two years, anyway. After that we tended to copy ourselves a bit much—but during those first two seasons we did some pretty wild stuff.

"I loved *Stingray*. I really wish that one would have made it. And I love *Wiseguy*."

"Hell, I love 'em all."

CHAPTER EIGHT:

The Gang's All Here

STUART MARGOLIN

He's probably best known as an actor—a performer who has made a career of playing seedy little schemers like Angel Martin of *The Rockford Files*.

But Stuart Margolin is a man whose talent defies being pigeonholed into only one such category.

Simply put, Margolin is a jack-of-all-trades and a master of many. Aside from Margolin the actor, there's also Margolin the director, Margolin the writer, Margolin the composer, Margolin the producer.

"Stuart Margolin's a remarkable man." said Meta Rosenberg. "l think he can do anything."

Said Margolin: "If I could be only one thing, I think I'd want to be a writer—that is, if I could make a living solely as a writer. But actually I enjoy doing a lot of different things. I suppose I'll keep on that way as long as they let me."

Indeed, Margolin—born on Jan. 31, 1940, in Davenport, Iowa, but raised in Dallas—made his first mark not as an actor, but as a playwright. His one-act play. *Sad Choices*, was produced off-Broadway in 1960, making him one of the youngest authors ever to have his work displayed on the New York stage.

Other of Margolin's seemingly unlikely screen credits, meanwhile, include *The Ballad of Andy Crocker* (1969), a made-for-TV movie for which he served as screenwriter, and *Evil Roy Slade* (1972), a motion picture for which he wrote the music score. And in *The Glitter Dome*, a 1984 made-for-cable movie, he demonstrated his versatility by wearing all the hats at once, serving as actor, director, producer and composer.

Still, it was his acting that represented his first and steadiest source of employment.

His earliest film and television credits came in 1966, with guest spots on TV series such as *Blue Light* and *Hey, Landlord*, a part in a warped "B" picture *Women of the Prehistoric Planet*, and a regular role in *Occasional Wife*, a short-lived situation comedy. And for nearly another decade, until truly standing out as Angel, Jim Rockford's shifty sidekick in *The Rockford Files*, Margolin moved from supporting role to supporting role with workmanlike efficiency, rarely attracting much notice but always staying busy.

"I'm a character actor," he said. "Many times if a character actor's done his job particularly well, you don't even notice him."

In those years, in fact, perhaps Margolin most closely was associated with his weekly appearances on *Love, American Style* (1969-73), a comedy anthology in which he appeared not in a recurring role but as one of the series' repertory players in a series of comic skits.

That started to change, however, when Margolin linked up with James Garner in *Nichols*, a 1971-72 Western series in which he played Mitch, a larcenous deputy sheriff who made Garner's underhanded character seem rather noble by comparison.

It was his performance on *Nichols*, in fact, that landed Margolin the role in *The Rockford Files*— and it was a flair for comic seaminess that made Angel one of the most memorable characters in the history of television.

"When you talk about *The Rockford Files*," said Rosenberg, "the second most important character—after Jim's, of course—had to be Stuart Margolin's."

Indeed, as the series progressed, Margolin's characterization became increasingly more offbeat and more involved in the shows. And in each of Rockford's last two seasons (1978-79 and 1979-80) Margolin was honored as television's best supporting actor in a drama series.

And while Margolin's on-screen shenanigans as Angel Martin brought him wider name recognition as an actor, his behind-the-scenes pursuits were paying big dividends as well.

"About the time that Rockford started, I was wanting to direct," he said. "We had lunch—Jim, Meta and I—and they told me about this part they had in mind for me. I said. yes, I'll do the two-hour (the movie pilot) and if that led to other things, fine.

"But I didn't want to be tied to the series week in and week out, because I was interested in directing."

That was why Margolin limited his on-screen involv*The Rockford Files* to a mere 29 episodes.

Other than directing "two-and-a-half" Rockford installments—"there was one episode where they needed another 10 minutes shot and I did it"—

Margolin balanced his semi-regular role as Angel with numerous behind-the-camera endeavors. They included: *The Texas Wheelers* (1974). *The Mary Tyler Moore Show* (1975), *Phyllis* (1975), *Wonder Woman* (1976), *Sara* (1976), *The Love Boat* (1977), *The Hardy Boys Mysteries* (1977) and a handful of TV movies—*Suddenly, Love* (1978), *Young Guy Christian* (1979) and *A Shining Season* (1979).

He also turned heads with his performance as Rabbi David Small in *Lanigan's Rabbi* (1976), a made-for-TV movie in which he and co-star Art Carney were so good a short-lived mystery series was spawned (although another actor, Bruce Solomon, played the rabbi in the series).

After Rockford, Margolin appeared as a regular in *Bret Maverick* (1981-82), again as one of Garner's offbeat sidekicks, in *Mr. Smith* (1983) and in a handful of motion pictures—*S.O.B.* (1981), *Class* (1983), *Running Hot* (1984) and *A Fine Mess* (1986).

Mostly, however, he plied his craft throughout the '80s as a television director. His post-Rockford directing credits include episodes of *Bret Maverick*, *Crazy Like A Fox*, *The Facts of Life*, *Growing Pains* and *The Tracy Ullman Show*.

Aside from *The Glitter Dome*, his most notable movie-length directorial credits include *The Long Summer of George Adams* (1982), which starred Garner, was produced by Rosenberg and was written by Rockford producer David Chase, and *The Room Upstairs* (1987), which starred Sam Waterson and Stockard Channing.

In late 1990, meanwhile, Margolin returned to series television as an actor, co-starring with Rosemary Dunsmore in *Mom, P.I.*, a light-hearted buddy-detective series made for the Canadian CBC.

In spite of his lengthy and wide-ranging resume, however, there's no escaping the fact that Angel Martin is the acting credit he's best remembered for.

"I can't exactly say that Angel represented my best work as an actor." he said. "There are other things I've done that I've been proud of too. But it is the role I'm most identified with, the one the public responded to most.

"And I'm not complaining, either. *The Rockford Files* was a show I enjoyed doing very much. I'm very proud of it."

NOAH BEERY JR.

"I was born in the (acting) business. I couldn't have gotten out of it if I'd wanted to."

So said Noah Beery, the longtime character actor perhaps best remembered for his role as Joseph "Rocky" Rockford in *The Rockford Files*. And he wasn't exaggerating in the slightest.

His father, Noah Beery Sr., was one of the great motion picture villains, "king of the bad guys." His uncle, Wallace Beery, was an Academy Award-winning character actor (for *The Champ*) with a flair for gruff-but-lovable types.

Beery, born in New York City Aug. 10, 1913, joined the family business at an early age, traveling with his parents in a stock company and even playing a part at age 7 in *The Mark of Zorro*, a 1920 silent that starred his father and Douglas Fairbanks.

Beery's acting career ultimately would span six decades, until his retirement in the mid-1990s. He appeared in more than 125 film features, a great number of them Westerns, and held regular roles in seven television series.

"No matter what anybody says, it's fun," he said. "Even when it's lousy, it's fun."

Dubbed "Pidge" by Josie Cohan, the sister of songwriter- entertainer George M. Cohan shortly after his birth (a nickname that has stuck his entire life), Beery was exposed to the business from day one. When he was a small boy, his family lived in Hollywood proper. Family friends were other show business pioneers. He attended school with the likes of Jesse Lasky Jr. and Douglas Fairbanks Jr.

After graduating from North Hollywood High School, he embarked on a solo film career in the 1930s, appearing mostly in serials. "It seemed as if they'd always make the aviation pictures, where you had to wear a leather coat and helmet, in the hot summer," he recalled. "And in the winter they'd make the jungle pictures, where you ran around in a breechcloth."

In the early going he often played the heroic leading man, but with *Tailspin Tommy* (1934) he found his niche as the hero's sidekick.

"I established an image long ago of being the brother of the girl or the friend of the leading man," he said. "If you want to keep busy (as an actor), don't be a Romeo."

Among the more notable films in which he appeared: *Of Mice and Men* (1939), Lon Chaney Jr.'s tour de force; *Sergeant York* (1941), an Oscar winner for Gary Cooper; *Red River* (1948), the John Wayne classic; *The Story of Will Rogers,* starring Will Rogers Jr.; *The Spirit of St. Louis* (1957), a James Stewart classic; *Inherit the Wind* (1960), starring Spencer Tracy, and *Walking Tall* (1973), with Joe Don Baker.

Beery singled out *Red River*, one of director Howard Hawks' finest films, as his favorite. "I love the West—and working in *Red River* was like living it, like really being on that cattle drive. I could have stayed on that picture forever."

His love of the West, perhaps, even outweighs his love of acting. In 1953, when the San Fernando Valley became too urbanized for his likes, he moved north to a ranch near the Mojave Desert, where he and his family have lived ever since.

He's a collector—not only of movie memorabilia, but also of Western paintings and sculptures. Moreover, his own sculptures sell well in Western galleries.

Beery made the move to television when the medium was still young.

After appearing in a number of one-shot parts, his first regular role on television was as Joey, the kind-hearted clown who cared for the young lead of *Circus Boy* (1956-58). He later appeared alongside Darren McGavin in *Riverboat* (1960-61), Ralph Taeger in *Hondo* (1967) and James Franciscus in *Doc Elliot* (1974).

It wasn't until after his 60th birthday, however. that Beery achieved true celebrity, cast as Jim Rockford's affable, blue- collar father in *The Rockford Files*.

"Old Pidge is a real pro," said James Garner. "He's so easy to work with, always prepared, always knows his lines."

"We always wanted Noah for the part, even when he wasn't available because of *Doc Elliot*," said Stephen Cannell. "With Noah and Jim, the chemistry couldn't have been better."

Indeed, in his six years as Garner's sidekick, Beery was nominated for three "best supporting actor" Emmys (1976-77, 1978-79 and 1979-80), the last two times being aced out by fellow Rockford regular Stuart Margolin.

After Rockford, Beery appeared in *The Quest* (1982), a series in which Cannell served as executive producer, and *The Yellow Rose* (1983-84), a Western soap opera.

He now spends his years of retirement on his Clear Creek-B Ranch.

Said Beery: "I'll take living in the country (any day)."

JOE SANTOS

"I never had dreams as a kid about becoming an actor. All I ever cared about was sports."

Indeed, although he has plied his trade as an actor for more two decades, Joe Santos' first love was—and still is—football.

"I got into acting quite by accident."

Santos, perhaps best remembered by television audiences for his role as Sergeant Dennis Becker on *The Rockford Files*, was born in Brooklyn June 8, 1931. A career in acting is a notion that didn't occur to him until well after his 30th birthday.

Santos always wanted to play football. He was a skills Position Player in high school.

"Quarterback, halfback, fullback. You name it, I played them all. I busted heads."

He attended Fordham University in the Bronx on a football scholarship during the 1949-50 academic year. He was a first stringer. The next year, 1950-51, he played for Miami of Ohio.

His goal was the pros, even though he now admits he was neither good enough or big enough.

"I was too dumb to know it at the time," he said.

Then a knee injury, not unlike the one that stymied James Garner's football days at Oklahoma, ended Santos' college career.

He served in the Army Medical Corps from 1952 to 1954 and over the next few years held a variety of odd jobs—he owned a bar, worked on the railroad. chopped down trees, delivered U.S.-made automobiles to Cuba—all the while holding out hope for a career as football player.

He wound up playing semi-pro football and laboring as a construction worker to make ends meet.

"I played for an all-black team for a while," he said, "everybody but me, of course. We'd travel from town to town—New York, New Jersey, Connecticut—and we'd play for a piece of the gate."

Santos didn't give acting a try until the mid-1960s and even then the impulse to do so wasn't his.

"A friend of mine was in this showcase (theater) and I had tagged along to watch," he said. "I was playing semi-pro ball at the time and I had a knee operation. I was still recuperating. So, anyway, this guy who was running the showcase for some reason had the insane idea of putting me on stage.

"Trust me, it was not successful."

But Santos was hooked, nonetheless.

While still toiling away as a construction worker, he would fit the showcase in with his semi-pro football. And before long he would take the plunge headlong.

"One day I came home and out of the blue I said, 'I'm gonna be an actor.' Well my wife (Mary, to whom he was married 1958 to 1989, when she died), she just about fell over. I quit my construction job."

His first job: a two-day role on *The Doctors*, a daytime soap opera, came almost instantly, but the next three years were lean indeed. Santos was forced to make ends meet working as a cabbie.

Then, in 1970, he got his big break, a part in *Panic in Needle Park*.

Santos had struck up a friendship with Al Pacino while playing softball in New York.

"Al recommended me for this part in the movie and Marion Dougherty—she was the casting director—had me read for the role of Al's brother." Santos said. "It turned out somebody else got that part, but Marion said she had this other role, a smaller one, she'd like me to do.

"Well, I was about to turn it down. I was very independent in those days, still am. But Marion said it could be worthwhile. So I did it and other things sort of fell in place after that. Marion was extremely kind to me. If any person gets credit for helping my career in those early days it was Marion Dougherty."

Soon thereafter came roles in *The Gang that Couldn't Shoot Straight* (1971), in which Santos played, not surprisingly, a New York crook; *Shamus* (1973), a crime story starring Burt Reynolds, and *The Friends of Eddie Coyle* (1973), another gangster film.

Santos' tough-guy looks and thick New York accent made him perfect for such films.

His most significant pre-Rockford role, however, was as a cop. The project was *The Blue Knight*, a four-night miniseries, based on the Joseph Wambaugh novel, that aired Nov. 13-18, 1973. Playing Sergeant Cruz Segovia, Santos received third billing after star William Holden and Lee Remick.

The role put Santos on the Hollywood map—and soon thereafter come guest parts in such series as *Police Story* (he would be featured in seven episodes over the next four years) and *Toma*. It was his role as a Mafia hit man in the first episode of *Toma*, a series produced by Stephen Cannell, that led to his landing the part of Becker in *The Rockford Files*.

"Stephen was always very good to me," Santos said. "I remember (Roy) Huggins wanted me for some other part in a different *Toma* episode, one that wasn't as good as the part I ended up playing. It was Stephen who got me that role—and it was his doing that I got the part in *The Rockford Files*.

"I was still living in New York at the time. I really didn't want to do television then and I was flying back and forth from New York whenever I had something lined up. Stephen called me and said he's got a part in this new series he's doing and he thought I'd be right for it.'

Santos was right, all right. He even was nominated for a "best supporting actor" Emmy in 1979, the year Stuart Margolin won his first of two Emmys in that department.

"I loved Jimmy (Garner). I loved Stephen. I loved doing the show."

After Rockford ceased production in November l979, Santos landed his only starring role in *Me and Maxx*, a short-lived comedy that debuted on NBC March 22, 1980 For two months, in *Me and Maxx* was the lead-in to summer Rockford reruns.

Santos also would have regular roles in *a.k.a Pablo* in 1984 and as Lieutenant Frank Harper in *Hardcastle and McCormick*, another Cannell series. In 1985-86. He had a recurring role as Lieutenant Nolon Page in *Magnum, P.I.* 1987-88.

Other notable post-Rockford credits, meanwhile, include *Power*, a 1980 made-for-TV movie starring Joe Don Baker, *Blue Thunder*, a 1983 action picture starring Roy Scheider, and *Fear City*, a 1985 film starring Tom Berenger and Billy Dee Williams.

More recently, Santos has spent the bulk of his time writing an autobiography. "It's my first book—and probably my last."

Reflecting on his past, he said he's happy he made the mid- life career change.

"I'm glad I did it. It's been a battle and a struggle, but I'm glad I did it. Acting's a lot harder than construction work.

"But it's also a lot more rewarding."

GRETCHEN CORBETT

There can be no doubt that television viewers know her best as attorney Beth Davenport from *The Rockford Files*.

But the body of Gretchen Corbett's work has taken place on the stage—not on TV or in motion pictures.

Corbett was born in Camp Sherman, Ore., Aug 13, 1947, and attended the Carnegie Institute of Technology.

Before reaching her 20th birthday, she made her professional debut as an actress, appearing as Desdemona in the Oregon Shakespeare Festival's 1967 production of *Othello*. In the seven years that followed, before landing her regular role on *The Rockford Files*, Corbett would appear in more than a dozen other stage productions, in some of them as the star.

She joined a repertory theater in New Orleans in 1967—playing, among other roles. Juliet in *Romeo and Juliet*—and made her New York debut shortly thereafter (August 1967), succeeding Jacqueline Coslow as Louka in the Sheridan Square Playhouse's production of *Arms and the Man*.

Her Broadway debut, in turn, came a mere two months later, when she played Sonya in *After the Rain* at the John Golden Theater.

Other productions in which Corbett starred in the years that followed: Iphigenia in *Aulis* (the title role), *The Bench, Forty Carats, The Unknown Soldier and His Wife, Henry VI, Part 2*, Shaw's *St. Joan* (as Joan of Arc), *The Survival of St. Joan*, (again, as Joan), *The Justice Box, The Ef-*

fect of Gamma Rays on Man-In-The- Moon Marigolds, As You Like It and *The Master Builder.*

Corbett's television debut, meanwhile came in 1968 when she appeared in an episode of *NYPD* and her first motion picture was *Out of It*, a 1969 comedy co-starring Jon Voight and Barry Gordon. In 1971, she appeared in *Let's Scare Jessica to Death.*

Becoming a contract player for Universal Studios in the early 1970s, she played a number of guest roles on series such as *Banacek, Gunsmoke, Ghost Story, Columbo* and *Kojak* before becoming Jim Rockford's lady lawyer. It was a role she would play for four years until her commitment to *The Rockford Files* expired.

After her involvement in Rockford came a handful of other projects—on stage, screen and TV—but none quite so memorable.

Her stage work included *At the End of Long Island* (1978), *The Carmine Brothers,* Italian Food Products Corp.'s Annual Pasta Pageant (1982), *The Queannapowitt Quartet* (1983) and *The Traveler* (1987). Film roles included *The Other Side of the Mountain Part 2* (1977) and *Jaws of Satan* (1981).

TV movie roles were numerous as well: *The Savage Bees* (1976): *Secrets of Three Hungry Wives* (1978), *Mandrake* (1979), *She's Dressed to Kill* (1979), *High Ice* (1980), *Million Dollar Infield* (1982) and *North Beach* and *Rawhide* (1985).

Her only involvement as a regular in another series, meanwhile, was the short-lived *Otherworld*, a science fiction- "fugitive" adventure show co-starring Sam Groom. It aired for three months in 1985 before its cancellation.

OTHERS OF NOTE

TOM SELLECK—A mere two appearances on *The Rockford Files* as private investigator Lance White, the suavely polished, everything- comes-easy-for-him counterpart to hard-luck Jim Rockford, put Tom Selleck on the road to stardom.

Before Rockford, Selleck toiled away for nearly a decade in commercials and small roles, usually cast as a "hunk." But playing Lance White changed Selleck's image, demonstrated that he had a genuine flair for Rockford-style humor.

Universal Studios was so captivated by his performance, in fact, it built a show around him,

Magnum, P.I. Thomas Magnum, in turn, was to the 1980s what Jim Rockford was to the '70s, the TV detective who turned TV detective shows upside down. *Magnum, P.I.* lasted eight enormously successful seasons (1980-88), rating as high as No. 3 during the 1982-83 season.

Selleck since has moved on to motion pictures. Some of his more notable films include *Three Men and A Baby* (1987), *Her Alibi* (1989) and *Quigley Down Under* (1990).

According to Meta Rosenberg, incidentally, the Lance White character was written specifically for Selleck to play.

"Steve (Cannell) saw that he was a wonderful actor and wanted to use him somehow in the show," she said. "That's how Lance White came about. In this case the actor come first. Then a character was created for him."

DENNIS DUGAN—As 23-year-old P.I. Richie Brockelman, Dennis Dugan appeared on only two Rockfords. But his affable presence on the series—as well as his peculiar history on television—make him well worth mentioning.

Richie Brockelman, for starters. was the only supporting Rockford character to "spin off" to his own series. Created by Stephen Cannell and Steven Bochco (of *Hill Street Blues/L.A. Law* fame), Brockelman first starred in a made-for-TV movie, *Richie Brockelman: The Missing 24 Hours* (1976).

Two years later the character resurfaced in a two hour Rockford episode, an episode that served as the jumping off point for his own series, *Richie Brockelman, P.I.* It lasted a mere five weeks and the following year Richie turned up again on Rockford.

Playing the budding gumshoe, meanwhile, was a youthful-looking 30-year-old who prior to Rockford had been featured in *Rich Man, Poor Man—Book I* (1976). Dugan also was a regular in *Empire* (1984) and *Shadow Chasers* (1985-86), but perhaps his most memorable TV role was as Captain Freedom in *Hill Street Blues.*

Dugan since has moved on to motion pictures. He appeared in *Parenthood* (1988) and *She's Having a Baby* (1989), among others, and made his directorial debut with *Problem Child* (1990).

RITA MORENO—Featured in three Rockford episodes as streetwalker Rita Capkovic, one show each year for the series' final three seasons, actress-dancer-singer Rita Moreno certainly made the most of her limited stay.

Twice she was nominated for best-supporting actress Emmys and once for her first Rockford performance, during the 1977-78 season, she won. She is one of the few entertainers to win all of show business' "Big Four" awards: She won an Academy Award for *West Side Story*, a Tony for *The Ritz*, a Grammy for the music from *The Electric Company* (an acclaimed PBS children's series in which she was a regular) and two Emmys (the second coming in 1977 for a guest spot on *The Muppet Show*.)

Her only other regular television role was in *9 to 5* (1982-83). Among the more notable movies in which she appeared, meanwhile: *Singin' in the Rain* (1952), *The King and I* (1956), *West Side Story* (1961), *Carnal Knowledge* (1971), *The Ritz* (1976) and *The Four Seasons* (1981).

ISAAC HAYES—Although his claim to fame is as a songwriter-arranger-vocalist-record producer, Isaac Hayes' appearances in three Rockford episodes as ex-con Gandy Fitch, the toughest man in San Quentin, were memorable indeed.

The first episode in which he appeared, *The Hammer of C Block* (that was what the fellow inmates called Gandy), Hayes stole the show as the recently released convicted killer who forced "Rockfish" to help find the man really responsible for the crime Gandy did 20 years for.

Gandy wasn't Hayes' only stab at acting, mind you. He also appeared in *Truck Turner* (1974), a picture for which he wrote the music score and played the title role, *Escape From New York* (1981*I'm Gonna Git You: Sucka* (1988): a parody of blaxploitation flicks.

Among his musical credits, meanwhile, are the Sam and Dave hits, "Soul Man" and "Hold On: I'm Coming," Carla Thomas' "B-A-B-Y," Johnnie Taylor's "I Had a Dream" and Dionne Warwick's "Deja Vu."

But his biggest claim to fame—and his biggest commercial hit—involved his music score for *Shaft*, a 1971 film starring Richard Roundtree. The double-album soundtrack brought Hayes an Academy Award, a Grammy, a No. 1 hit on the pop charts and platinum record sales.

JAMES LUISI—As Lieutenant Doug Chapman, James Luisi's gruff-and-unlovable character served as Rockford's favorite foil for four seasons (1976-80).

His was a character who genuinely disliked Rockford, bringing him nothing but grief. Yet when Chapman typically wound up one-upped by our hero, it made for delicious TV. His was a thankless job—and one he did particularly well.

Aside from numerous guest spots as cops and crooks on other detective shows, such as *Barnaby Jones* and *Cannon*, Luisi also had regular roles on *Harris and Company* (1979), a family drama, and *Renegades* (1983), a cop show.

He also won a daytime Emmy in 1976 for his role in *First Ladies' Diaries: Martha Washington*.

SIMON OAKLAND—As private eye Vern St. Cloud, Simon Oakland gave a wonderfully scuzzy performance, portraying in an occasional role a character so despicable he made Jim Rockford look like a Dudley Do Right.

Indeed, seamy crabbiness was Simon Oakland's stock in trade. He hollered endlessly as Inspector Spooner, the hero's boss in *Toma* (1973-74). He hollered even more as editor Tony Vincenzo, the hero's boss in *Kolchak: The Night Stalker* (1974-75). The same was true when he played a general in *Baa Baa Black Sheep* (1976-76) and a police sergeant in *David Cassidy, Man Undercover* (1978).

Some notable motion pictures in which Oakland appeared, large roles and small, include *Psycho* (1960), *The Satan Bug* (1965). *The Sand Pebbles* (1966) and *Bullitt* (1968).

In spite of his tough-guy persona, Oakland (who died Aug. 29, 1983) had a gentler side. He was on accomplished violinist.

BO HOPKINS—Although Gretchen Corbett left the series after four seasons. Jim Rockford still needed the services of an attorney from time to time.

The choice was Bo Hopkins, whose character, John Cooper, was a disbarred lawyer who could only do legal research but still had a few connections. He appeared in three episodes during the 1978-79 season.

Hopkins had roles in three other TV series—*Doc Elliot* (1974), *Aspen* (1977) and *Dynasty* (1981)—but he's probably better known as a motion picture presence, usually playing second leads or major supporting characters.

Some of his more notable films: *The Wild Bunch* (1969), his motion picture debut; *The Getaway* (1971), a film in which James Garner did some uncredited stunt driving, and *American Graffiti* (1973).

KATHRYN HARROLD—In a mere two Rockford episodes, in the role of blind psychologist Megan Dougherty, the character played by lovely Kathryn Harrold represented the closest Jim Rockford ever came to true love—and lost love.

Harrold's only regular roles in series television, meanwhile, were as police Officer Jenny Loud of *MacGruder and Loud* (1985) and high school teacher Sara Newhouse in *The Bronx Zoo* (1987-88).

This page: Joe Santos
Opposite page:
Gretchen Corbett

CHAPTER NINE:

BEHIND THE CAMERAS

ROY HUGGINS

"I went into television for a very specific reason. In movies the director was king. But television—that was a producer's medium."

And as Roy Huggins saw it, he could realize the freedom, the control and the monetary rewards more fully as a television producer. He was right.

Huggins, born July 18, 1914, in Litelle, Wash., worked as an industrial engineer in the 1940s before making his mark as a writer of novels and short stories.

It was his first novel, in fact, a crime yarn called *The Double Take*, that opened the door to motion pictures. Columbia Pictures bought film rights to the book—the 1948 film was titled *I Love Trouble*—and director S. Sylvan Simon brought Huggins in to write the script.

In the years that followed he wrote the stories or scripts for a number of other films, many of them Westerns. Among them: *Fuller Brush Man* (1948), *Too Late for Tears* (1949), *The Lady Gambles* (1949), *Woman in Hiding* (1949), *The Good Humor Man* (1950), *Sealed Cargo* (1961), *Hangman's Knot* (1962), *Gun Fury* (1963), *Pushover* (1964) and *Three Hours to Kill* (1964).

Of those, *Hangman's Knot*, the film that also represented Huggins' directorial debut, stands out the most. Starring Randolph Scott, Donna Reed and a very young Lee Marvin, it is regarded as one of Scott's best films.

In 1955, however, Huggins moved to television—and in doing so became a behind-the-scenes star.

His first success was as the producer/creator/writer of *Cheyenne*, a Western starring Clint Walker that was a consistent ratings topper, enduring eight seasons. The following year Huggins brought us *Conflict* (1956-57), an anthology, and the year after that he created *Colt .45* (1957-60).

Outshining *Colt .45*, however, and commanding the bulk of his attention, was *Maverick*, the series that made James Garner a star while throwing TV Western fans a curve. By its second season: *Maverick* had bucked the odds (it had been placed in a doomingly difficult time slot, opposite Jack Benny, Ed Sullivan and Steve Allen) by placing No. 6 in the all-important Nielsen ratings.

As *Maverick* was on the rise, meanwhile, Huggins helped create *77 Sunset Strip* (1958-64), the hip private eye series starring Efrem Zimbalist Jr., Roger Smith and Edd "Kooky" Byrnes. (Stuart Bailey, the name of Zimbalist's character, also had been the hero's name in Huggins' *The Double Take*.)

After putting *Maverick* over the top, however, Huggins left the series and also parted ways with Warner Brothers.

"I rarely stay with a series more than one or two years," he said. "*Maverick* was no exception. It took me a year to get out of my contract at Warners. That done, I went home, sat down on my patio and had the most productive hour of my life."

In that hour, he penciled out the premise for *The Fugitive*, a series that would take two years before finding its way to television, but would become an enormous success. The famous final episode of the David Janssen "man-on-the-run" series (Aug. 29, 1967) was seen by more viewers than any single episode of a series to that date.

Huggins' ties to the series, however, were only in getting the ball rolling—for he sold the TV rights to *The Fugitive* to Quinn Martin, who served as executive producer.

"I was busy working on my Ph.D. at UCLA at the time," he said. "It was something I had promised myself I would do for 20 years."

Once that was accomplished, Huggins returned to television with *Run for Your Life* (1965-68), an anthology of sorts in which Ben Gazzara, a lawyer suffering from an incurable disease, saw the world—cramming a lifetime of adventure into his few remaining years.

There were still other series in the years that followed: *The Outsider* (1968-69), starring Darren McGavin; the "Lawyers" segment of *The Bold Ones* (1969-72); *Alias Smith and Jones* (1971-73), an offbeat Western, and *Toma* (1973-74).

During the 1974-75 season, meanwhile, he played an important role in the development of *The Rockford Files*. It was under his production company, Public Arts, and for his *Toma* that the Rockford character and series was first conceived.

Moreover, it was Huggins' story from which Stephen Cannell wrote the first Rockford script, the movie pilot. He also wrote the stories for the bulk of the first season's episodes. His work in that capacity appeared under the pen name John Thomas James, one of more than a dozen he has used through the years. (Huggins said the pen name derives from the names of three of his sons—John, Thomas and James.)

True to his track record in series television, however, Huggins' ties to *The Rockford Files* lasted no further than that first season.

Since Rockford, his credits have included *Baretta* (1975-78), the Robert Blake series that rated as high as No. 8 in the 1975-76 season; *The Captains and the Kings* (1976-77); *Aspen* (1979); *The Last Convertible* (1981); the *Blue Thunder* TV series (1984); and *Hunter*, the Cannell series for which he broke his self-imposed two-years-to-a-series rule by serving as executive producer for three seasons.

In 1990 he was to serve as executive producer for a motion picture version of *The Fugitive*, a 1991 film starring Alec Baldwin in the Dr. Richard Kimble role that David Janssen first made famous.

Despite the lengthy list of film and television credits, he has no trouble singling out a favorite.

"It's *Maverick*, without a doubt. Kaiser (Aluminum, the series sponsor) had put us in an impossible spot, against three of the biggest shows on television, and it was great just watching *Maverick* climb and climb in the ratings in spite of the competition.

"I had the time of my life doing that series."

His second and third favorites, he added, are *The Rockford Files* and *Run for Your Life*.

"I love television," he said. "It's been good to me."

META ROSENBERG

Ask Meta Rosenberg about her fondest memory from *The Rockford Files* and she'll tell you how, to this day, fans persist in their devotion to the series.

"People often tell me it was their favorite show," she said. "They don't know me, but they recognize my name from the credits. It's been more than 10 years since we quit making *The Rockford Files* and they still do it.

"I find that very gratifying. To have been involved in a show that people love that much— well, I'll always cherish that."

Rosenberg served six seasons with *The Rockford Files* in the capacity of executive producer. "I was in charge," she said. "It was a great show to work on, a fun show."

In addition to her duties, which included all the casting for the series, Rosenberg directed a half dozen episodes, her first being *A Portrait of Elizabeth* during the second season.

Rosenberg would hold that lofty executive producer title for only two other television series, both of them starring James Garner— *Nichols* (1971-7Z) and *Bret Maverick* (1981-82). The reason is that Rosenberg's professional career and Garner's have been, for the most part, one and the same.

Rosenberg was Garner's agent in the 1950s. They were together during Garner's *Maverick* days, during his well-publicized feud and lawsuit with Warner Brothers that ended his ties to that series and throughout the 1960s, when he starred in nearly 20 motion pictures.

During that span she became his partner at Cherokee Productions, Garner's production company. Thus, when Garner returned to television to make *Nichols*, he considered it only natural that she be his executive producer.

The same was true later for *The Rockford Files* and *Bret Maverick.*

Rosenberg since has produced a number of television movies, the most notable of which came shortly after Rockford. Those include *Off the Minnesota Strip* (1960), a film scripted by Rockford alumnus David Chase, and *The Long Summer of George Adams* (1982), a film starring Garner and directed by Stuart Margolin, which represents one of Garner's best post-Rockford performances.

Curiously, however, even though *The Rockford Files* rates as Rosenberg's most significant television credit—as her 1978 Emmy attests—she doesn't readily rate it as her favorite series.

"Rockford was wonderful," she said. "But I was also very fond of *Nichols*, as Jim was. If you asked me to pick a favorite between the two, I'm afraid I simply couldn't do it."

OTHERS OF NOTE

CHARLES FLOYO JOHNSON—Althouph perhaps best known as a producer with such series as *The Rockford Files* and *Magnum, P.l.*, Charles Floyd Johnson didn't start out in television.

He knows the medium, to be sure, but Johnson also is an attorney and an expert on copyright law.

A Vietnam veteran, having served in the Army from 1965 to 1967, Johnson passed the bar in Washington, D.C., in 1968 and began a career in law. From 1967 to 1970 he was an advisor in the U.S. Copyright Office in Washington and in 1971 was an associate in the Howard Berg Law Offices in Wilmington, Del. He is the author of *Copyright and Developing Countries*, published in 1967.

Then he made an unlikely move to television, first as a production coordinator for Universal Television (1971-74), a job that led directly to his production duties on *The Rockford Files*, for which in 1978 he collected one of his two Emmys.

His first Rockford credit, however, was not in the capacity of a producer, but as a writer. *The Deep Blue Sleep*, one of his few story credits, was telecast during the series' second season. The following year, 1976-77, he and David Chase joined the Rockford production team.

After *The Rockford Files*, Johnson served as producer for *Bret Maverick* (1981-82), as supervising producer for *Magnum, P.I.* (from the years 1982 to 1986) and ultimately as Magnum's co-executive producer (1986-88). He produced a 1981-82 PBS series *Voices of the People* (In Celebration of Black Poetry).

DAVID CHASE—Although he won the first of his two Emmys in the capacity of a producer, David Chase is first and foremost a writer.

Chase, who served as producer of *The Rockford Files* for three years (1976-79), contributed mostly to the writing end of the series. He wrote the stories or scripts for 17 episodes, including three of the final season's 10 episodes, even though he had left his role of producer after the 1978-79 season.

Among his most memorable scripts were *Black Mirror* and *Love Is the Word* (both featuring Rockford's love interest, Megan Dougherty) and *The Queen of Peru.*

Chase first started to attract notice as a television writer while penning scripts for *The Magician* (1970-71). Other television credits of note include *Kolchak The Night Stalker* (1974-75) and *Switch* (1976-78), shows for which he served as story editor, and *The Misadventures of Sheriff Lobo* (1979-81).

JUANITA BARTLETT—She broke into the business at Cherokee Productions as Meta Rosenberg's secretary. Less than a decade later she achieved producer status with *The Rockford Files.*

Writer Juanita Bartlett's big break came in 1971, when Rosenberg and James Garner were involved in the making of *Nichols.* Bartlett submitted a script to producer Frank Pierson and soon thereafter her days as a secretary were behind her.

"I was really a writer with a drawer full of rejection slips until then)," she said.

With *The Rockford Files* all that changed. Writing regularly for the series from the very beginning, she soon held the title of executive story editor. She served as producer during the series' final season, filling the void left by David Chase's departure.

In all, she was involved in writing the scripts or stories for 34 episodes, more than a third of the series' total output and second only to Stephen Cannell's 38.

Perhaps her most memorable Rockford creation was prostitute Rita Capkovic. Rita Moreno, who played the character in three episodes, each written by Bartlett, won an Emmy.

Since then, Bartlett's ties to series involving Garner or Stephen Cannell have been numerous. Her other writing/production credits include *The New Maverick*, a TV movie (1978), *Stone* (1980), *Tenspeed and Brown Shoe* (1980), *Bret Maverick* (1981-82), *The Greatest American Hero* (1981-83), *The Quest* (1982), *Scarecrow and Mrs. King* (1983-87), *Spenser: For Hire* (1985-88).

She also formed her own production company, The Juanita Bartlett Company, and oversees production for *In The Heat of the Night,* a popular police series starring Carroll O'Connor and Harold Rollins.

MIKE POST—His name and his face might not be widely recognized by television viewers, but his work is unmistakable.

Musician Mike Post and Pete Carpenter, a long-time collaborator, were contributors of one of the most distinctive elements of *The Rockford Files,* its zesty theme music.

In fact, the tune, simply titled *The Rockford Files,* was a hit, reaching No. 10 on the Billboard charts in 1975.

Other chart-topping TV theme songs by Post include *Believe It Or Not* (from *The Greatest American Hero, No. 2,* (1981), the theme to *Hill Street Blues* (No. 10 in 1982) and the theme to *Magnum P.I.* (No. 25, 1982). He also wrote the themes to such series as *The A-Team, Stingray* and *L.A. Law,* as well as the tunes in the 1990 musical drama, *Cop Rock.*

Still others may remember Post from his years on *The Andy Williams Show* (1969-71) and *The Mac Davis Show* (1974-76). In each series he was the leader of the Mike Post Orchestra.

James Garner with Kathryn Harrold from "Love is the Word" episode of THE ROCKFORD FILES

CHAPTER TEN:

AT THE EMMY'S

James Garner wins an Emmy

"Jim Garner doesn't get enough credit as an actor. He makes it look so easy."

So said Meta Rosenberg—and she'll get no argument here.

But there was one night, Sept. 11, 1977, when Garner finally got the acclaim he so richly deserved for his work on *The Rockford Files*.

On that Sunday evening he was named television's best dramatic actor. He won an Emmy.

The series would lay claim to four more Emmy statuettes over the next three seasons, however Garner's triumph was a first—for the actor as well as the series.

But when the winner was announced, Garner wasn't there to collect his prize.

"Jim's a shy person, you understand," Rosenberg said. "He doesn't like to be interviewed, doesn't like to give speeches. He feels terribly uncomfortable in those situations—and that was why he didn't attend (the awards ceremony)."

After the announcement was made, Rosenberg, Stephen Cannell, Charles Floyd Johnson and David Chase—all of whom attended - - rushed to a telephone to give Garner the news.

Garner's reaction was one of astonished surprise. "Oh, my God," he said.

"The next day," Rosenberg recounted for *TV Guide* , "the crew and the regulars gave a party for him. They told him he had to make a speech. 'I can't,' he said. 'You gotta,' they said.

"Then he did. 'I don't believe in actors getting awards. I'm embarrassed to win an award for working with the people I love the most.'

"Then he cried. So did everyone else."

Here, then, is a list of the series' Emmy winners and nominations. After nary a nomination its first year, the series had 17 nominations and five winners over the next five.

1975-76

One nomination.

James Garner, outstanding lead actor in a drama series.

Winner: Peter Falk, *Columbo*.

1976-77

Two nominations, one winner (James Garner).

James Garner, winner for outstanding lead actor in a drama series.

(Other nominees: Robert Blake, *Baretta*; Peter Falk, *Columbo*; Jack Klugman, *Quincy, M.E.*; Karl Malden, *The Streets of San Francisco*.

Noah Beery, outstanding continuing performance by a supporting actor in a drama series.

Winner: Gary Frank, *Family*.

1977-78

Three nominations, two winners (best series and Rita Moreno).

The Rockford Files, winner for outstanding drama series.

(Other nominees: *Columbo, Family, Lou Grant, Quincy, M.E.* Awards went to producers Meta Rosenberg, Stephen J. Cannell, David Chase and Charles Floyd Johnson.)

James Garner, outstanding lead actor in a drama series.

Winner: Ed Asner, *Lou Grant*.

Rita Moreno, winner for outstanding lead actress for a single appearance in a drama or comedy series, an episode titled *The Paper Palace*.

(Other nominees: Patty Duke Astin, *Having Babies*; Kate Jackson, *James at 15*; Jayne Meadows, *Meeting of the Minds*; Irene Tedrow, *James at 15*.)

1978-79

Six nominees, one winner (Stuart Margolin).

The Rockford Files, outstanding drama series.

Winner: *Lou Grant*.

James Garner, outstanding lead actor in a drama series.

Winner: Ron Liebman, *Kaz*.

Stuart Margolin, winner for outstanding supporting actor in a drama series.

(Other nominees: Noah Beery, *The Rockford Files*; Joe Santos, *The Rockford Files*; Mason Adams, *Lou Grant*; Robert Walden, *Lou Grant*.)

Rita Moreno, outstanding lead actress in a drama series.

Winner: Mariette Hartley, *The Incredible Hulk*.

1979-80

Five nominees, one winner (Stuart Margolin):

The Rockford Files, outstanding drama series.

Winner: *Lou Grant*.

Stuart Margolin, winner for outstanding supporting actor in a drama series.

(Other nominees: Noah Beery, *The Rockford Files*; Mason Adams, *Lou Grant*; Robert Walden, *Lou Grant*)

Lauren Bacall and Mariette Hartley, outstanding lead actress in a drama series. (Bacall for *Lions, Tigers, Monkeys and Dogs*; Hartley for *Paradise Cove*.)

Winner: Barbara Bel Geddes, *Dallas*

James Garner in SPACE

STORIES

CHAPTER ELEVEN:

ROCKFORD'S FIRST CASE

If his Yellow Pages ad is to be believed, Jim Rockford's first case probably came in 1968, when the Rockford Agency presumably opened for business.

As far as television viewers are concerned, however, his first case that really mattered was the Harvey Butler murder probe of 1974, an investigation documented in the movie pilot of *The Rockford Files*. The 90-minute movie of the same title was telecast on NBC March 27, 1974.

In many respects it was Rockford's most important case—not because of any particulars from the investigation, but because it was here that the foundation for the series was laid. *The Rockford Files* pilot started a ball rolling that wouldn't slow down for six years.

Jim Rockford's not-so-traditional approach to the detective business? That was established here. His hard-luck relationship with non-paying clients, rough-and-tumble bad guys and belligerent police? That was established here. His friendships with Rocky, Becker and Angel? Those, too, were established here.

That being the case, the pilot movie merits a longer, more detailed look than any of the others:

THE ROCKFORD FILES

Director: Richard T. Heffron.

Writer: Stephen J. Cannell (from John Thomas James' story).

Executive producer: Jo Swerling Jr.

Producer: Stephen J. Cannell.

Music: Mike Post and Pete Carpenter

Art director: Robert Luthardt.

Photography: Lamar Boren

Cast: James Garner (Jim Rockford), Lindsay Wagner (Sara Butler), William Smith (Jerry Grimes), Nita Talbot (Mildred Elias), Joe Santos (Sergeant Dennis Becker), Stuart Margolin (Angel Martin), Robert Donley (Joseph "Rocky" Rockford), Pat Renella (Morrie Talbot), Bill Mumy (Nick Butler), Mike Steele (Danford Baker), Michael Lerner (Dr. Ruben Seelman), Ted Gehring (Norm Mitchell), Bill Quinn (Harvey Butler).

(Note: The film was re-titled *Backlash of the Hunter* when added to the series' syndication run. It appears as a two-part episode.)

An old derelict is brutally murdered at the beach. While waiting to meet someone beneath the Santa Monica pier, he is strangled with a necktie by a man who was following him.

It's a crime destined to receive only a cursory look from the police. Sergeant Dennis Becker would like to delve into the matter more deeply, but his boss, Captain Dell, considers the case unsolvable and a waste of time.

Becker: "I got a hunch there's more behind it than just a mugging."

Dell: "Dump it. We ain't got time for it."

So dump it Becker does, stuffing the Harvey Butler homicide file in the unsolved inactive drawer. And that would be that if not for the victim's daughter, Sara Butler, who seeks out private investigator Jim Rockford, hoping to hire him to look into the matter.

Sara: "I want to retain you, Mr. Rockford. I need help."

Rockford: "I hope you can afford me."

Sara: "But you haven't even heard what I want."

Rockford: "You're right. But if we could just talk about my fee first, we will probably save a lot of time. I cost $200 a day, plus expenses."

Sara: "$200?"

Rockford: "Plus expenses. And I only handle criminal cases that are closed. It's not like it is on TV. I get myself messed up in an LAPD active file and I get my can shot off, my license pulled and probably get booked for obstructing justice."

Sara: "Where did you get this wonderful finishing school approach?"

Rockford: "People come to me all the time. Sit right there where you're sitting and their eyes out. Old women who want their sons out of jail. Girlfriends, fathers—all of them with problems. I used to be a softie and listen and then we'd get around to the money and they couldn't pay, so they left and I'd be all depressed and that was that. It was turning me off on my business so now I do it this way."

So Sara crossly scribbles out a check for $200. Now she has his attention. She tells Rockford about her father's death, how the case has been dropped by the Los Angeles police, how Becker advised her to see Rockford, how she thinks she's stumbled onto a lead.

So Rockford tentatively accepts the case.

But before leaving his office he makes a private phone call: "I'd like to run a credit check on a Miss Sara Butler, 2378 Addison Street, Los Angeles."

Sara's lead involves her brother Nick, a drug store delivery boy. Nick refuses to talk—until Rockford threatens to get physical.

Nick: "You're a cop, hunh?"

Rockford: "What I am, sonny, is about 50 pounds heavier than you and one hell of a lot meaner. So you better soften up your approach or get ready to kiss the deck."

So Nick spills it. Seems a woman named Mildred Elias, to whom Nick makes deliveries, has inexplicably offered to put him through medical school. That's Sara's so-called lead, just an odd development that makes no sense.

Rockford agrees it's unusual—"but not that unusual."

In fact. Rockford's inclined to forget the case altogether, particularly after he learns that Sara can't afford to pay him.

Rockford: "I was just beginning to like you. I had some people run a credit check on you. You know what I found out?"

Sara: "What?"

Rockford: "You laid some bad paper on me. You're the only person in town with worse credit than me."

Sara: "What is it with you? Are you independently wealthy? Or on some kind of big case or something?"

Rockford: "If I don't think there's much chance of solving this case and I still go ahead and take everything you make in two weeks for one day of my time, what does that make me? An unprincipled jerk. So I don't take cases where I think I'm wasting my time or your money—that is if you had any."

But Rockford arrives at a compromise. He agrees to spend three hours on it. no charge. Then, if the case shows promise and if Sara can pony up 200 a day, he'll stay on it.

Rockford's three-hour preliminary investigation involves a visit to Angel Martin, who works in the library morgue of a city newspaper.

Rockford has Angel sift through old society columns for information on Mildred Elias. Angel finds that Nick Butler's would-be benefactor is a recent widow, that her elderly husband, a millionaire, died on their wedding night in Las Vegas several months before the murder of Harvey Butler.

It's a coincidence that arouses Rockford's curiosity.

Rockford may be onto something, but before proceeding, he wants assurance he'll be paid for his services. So that evening, over dinner, he and Sara resume haggling over money.

Sara: "Are you going to take the case or not?"

Rockford: "How are you going to pay for it?"

Sara: "I thought maybe we could work out a deal."

Rockford: "I'm sorry, but I don't have specials any more. It's got to be 200 a day, plus expenses."

Sara: "What if I could pay you on the installment plan?"

Rockford: "I did that once and got stiffed."

Sara: "I'm trying to hire you but I guess you just don't want to work for me."

Rockford: "you're not trying to hire me. You're trying to chisel me down."

But again, they reach a compromise, an installment plan in which Sara pays $25 a week. Rockford's on the case. And his new line of investigation takes him to Las Vegas, where he consults with the coroner who performed the autopsy on Mildred Elias' husband.

Dr. Seeiman assures Rockford that the death was by natural causes. "He'd been at the wedding party and he ate too much and drank too much—and he couldn't take it."

A dead end.

But after Rockford leaves, the doctor places a long-distance call to Mildred Elias, warning her someone is poking around into her husband's death again.

Mrs. Elias, in turn, places a call to a man named Jerry Grimes. Jerry is the man who strangled Sara's father.

"I've got to see you," she tells him. "I think we're in trouble."

When Rockford returns to Los Angeles, his first order of business is to see Sara, tell her he's off the case and hand her a bill for his time.

When he drives away, though, Jerry Grimes is following him.

And Rockford stays off the case for only a matter of minutes before an idea occurs to him. He pulls his car to the side of the road and calls Sara from a pay telephone.

Rockford: "I've been thinking there's still one other thing I could check out."

Sara: "What's wrong? Did you just figure out you're overdrawn at the bank?"

So he's back on the case again. His new tack involves a visit to Mrs. Elias. Wearing a tie and glasses—his sorry version of a disguise— Rockford poses as Carter Simpson, assistant dean of admissions at Mollar Medical School.

He pumps the woman for information regarding her plans to send Nick Butler to medical school. but her answers don't seem to get him anywhere.

But after Rockford leaves, Jerry Grimes, who had remained on Rockford's tail, confronts Mildred Elias.

Jerry: "What the hell was he doing here?"

Mrs. Elias: "His name is Simpson."

Jerry: "His name is Rockford. He's the guy you asked me to follow!"

Rockford has struck a nerve after all.

Back to Rockford, who's busy calling it quits again.

"Look, Sara," he says, handing her a new bill, "if Mrs. Elias had said anything I could get my teeth into, I would've kept on."

Sara: "This is the third time you've quit and I'm still getting these little slips of paper from you."

Rockford: "I'm off it for good."

Fat chance, for after parting with Sara, Rockford spots Jerry Grimes' car in his rear-view mirror.

Curious, he parks outside a bar and goes inside. Jerry follows him. Rockford heads for the men's room, where he removes the soap container from the wash basin, pours liquid soap on the floor and waits. After a time, Jerry walks in.

Rockford: "You got to be one of the dumbest-looking apes I ever saw."

Jerry moves quickly toward Rockford, preparing to make a savage karate kick, but he slips on the soap. Then Rockford socks him in the face, knocking the thug out cold.

Rockford opens his fist, revealing a roll of nickles.

When Jerry comes to, he finds himself bound at the feet with Rockford's belt and propped against a toilet. Rockford already has gone through his wallet.

Rockford: "You know what's wrong with karate,

Jerry? It's based on the ridiculous assumption that the other guy will fight fair."

Rockford asks why he was being followed, but Jerry isn't talking. And Rockford doesn't particularly press the matter. He merely gives up and leaves.

Moments later, when Jerry storms out of the bar and drives away, Rockford, already in his car, starts his engine and pulls out in pursuit.

Rockford tails Jerry to another bar, then hustles over to Sara Butler's house.

Rockford: "We got somebody interested in us. That means I turned over at least one of the right rocks. Get dressed in something sexy. I'm going to offer you a chance to get some of your money back."

Sara does as instructed and back they go to the bar Jerry stopped at. Rockford's plan is for Sara to pick up Jerry—and drug his drink.

Sara: "How much of my own money am I going to earn back?"

Rockford: "I usually pay my operatives 20 bucks an hour for this kind of thing."

Sara: "I won't do it for less than 50."

Rockford's getting a taste of his own medicine.

At the bar, Sara picks up Jerry and off they go to his place. Rockford follows.

In Jerry's apartment, he starts pawing her—but before he gets anywhere he blacks out. This gives Rockford the opportunity to enter the apartment and rummage through Jerry's things, in hopes of finding a lead.

Rockford: "Let's move quick. I don't want him to wake up and catch us."

Sara: "You aren't afraid of him, are you?"

Rockford: "You're damn right, I am."

Soon Rockford finds a photo of Mildred Elias. Now he knows there's a connection.

He just isn't sure yet what it is.

Next stop, Angel Martin and the newspaper morgue.

Rockford wants to see a photo of William Elias. Mrs. Elias' dead husband. He compares it to a photo of Harvey Butler. They don't look alike— yet Rockford thinks he's on to something.

During the visit, meanwhile, Angel drops a bombshell on Sara. "Jim and me go way back. We was in the pen together."

Rockford continues to piece things together, asking questions about her wino father's past.

Sara: "Once I couldn't find him for several weeks. I almost came apart because I was afraid he'd died and was buried someplace and I'd never know where."

After a long search, Sara adds, she eventually found him. "I took him home) and fed him some food and asked him where he'd been."

Rockford: "What'd he say?"

Sara: "He had gone to the desert for his health."

Rockford: "When was this?"

Sara: "It was June of last year."

Rockford: "In other words, the time he was missing was just about the time Elias died."

Jerry Grimes, meanwhile, has commissioned a Las Vegas hit man to commit two murders. Presumably, Rockford will be one of the victims.

The wheels are spinning on the Rockford front as well.

He phones his father, Rocky, whose buddy is a janitor in the city administrator's office in Las Vegas.

Rockford: "Does he have a set of keys. Can he let me into City Hall?"

Rocky: "I don't know."

Rockford: "I'll pay you 50 bucks."

Rocky agrees.

When Rockford hangs up, Sara says "You aren't having much of a day for profits. You already gave me 50 and now your father gets 50."

Rockford: "You're paying his 50. That's expenses."

Before Rockford and Sara head to Las Vegas, Rockford fetches his gun from a tin box in his desk drawer.

Sara: "You mean you didn't have a gun on you when I picked up Jerry? I thought you were carrying a gun."

Rockford: "I can't. I haven't got a permit to carry a gun."

Sara: "But you're a private investigator."

Rockford: 'You ought to see what you've got to go through downtown to get a permit to carry a concealed weapon. It's impossible. Nobody's got permits except the guys on TV—and I figure they don't really count."

When Rockford and Sara arrive at Las Vegas City Hall, it's still the wee hours. Rocky and his janitor friend are waiting and the janitor lets Rockford into the Civil Records office.

Rockford wants to find out who performed the marriage ceremony for Mr. and Mrs. Elias. He finds the name—Danford Baker—and flies.

Only trouble is he's too late. Jerry Grimes and his hired killer, Morrie Talbot, get to the preacher first and they spirit him away. Jerry pistol whips Baker in the process, killing him, and loads him into their getaway car just as Rockford drives up.

Rockford gives chase but he can't keep up. Jerry and Morrie manage to make it to a getaway plane and fly away before Rockford can catch them.

They dump the minister's body out of the plane into a lake.

Sara: "Will you explain it to me? What the hell is going on?"

Rockford: "Mildred and her $10 million bridegroom leave the wedding party in L.A., fly to Vegas, check into their motel—and Old Man Elias dies."

Sara: "Before the wedding?"

Rockford: "She calls Jerry Grimes and tells him she just lost 10 million bucks. Jerry says, 'You got all the papers signed—license, all that?' and Mildred says, 'Yeah, but he's dead.' And Jerry says, 'Sit tight, baby. Throw an electric blanket on him and keep him warm. I'll be there in two hours with a substitute."

Sara. "And he picked up my father?"

And he was killed when he tried to blackmail Mildred Elias.

Rockford and Sara aren't out of the woods yet though, because Talbot's plane takes a pass over Rockford's car—a strafing run in which Jerry takes potshots with a machine pistol. Jerry hits

Rockford's car, which shudders to a stop—and the plane is turning for another pass.

Rockford has no choice but to use his gun. He takes shots at the approaching plane, missing completely on its first run, but hitting it the next time.

The plane crashes and burns.

Rockford: "Was it worth it, Sara?"

Sara: "No."

At a Las Vegas police station, Rockford is being questioned by a cop.

Cop: "Where did you get it? You ain't go no permit to carry a gun."

Rockford: "Look, you're missing the point. Those guys probably killed a minister named Danford Baker."

Cop: "His body wasn't found in the wreckage."

Rockford: "What about the signature cards on the record book of the minister? Have you checked them against the marriage license?"

Cop: "We're doing that now. Meanwhile, I want to know where you got that gun. You may not know it, buster, but you can't go around shooting down light aircraft with hand guns."

During this haggling, Becker phones from Los Angeles to say he already has arrested Mildred Elias. And though Becker vouches for Rockford, the Vegas cop still intends to lock him up on a gun charge.

Sara: "I'm sorry about this. I feel responsible."

Rockford: "I'll only charge you half-price for the time I spend in jail."

Sara: "You're kidding?"

Rockford grins. "Yeah."

And the Las Vegas cop leads Rockford away to a jail cell—making him perhaps the first TV detective to solve a murder and wind up behind bars for his efforts.

James Garner with the stars of BRET MAVERICK, the television series that revived his character created more than 20 years ago: (left to right) Darleen Carr, Ed Bruce and Suart Margolin, who played Angel on ROCKFORD.

GARNER'S OTHER ROLES

Following is the documented case file of private investigator Jim Rockford.

The case load during his six-year stay on network television amounted to 114 episodes (including four two-parters). One episode, not telecast by the network, can be seen in syndication, as can the 90-minute movie pilot.

CAST
Jim Rockford: James Garner
Joseph "Rocky" Rockford : Noah Beery
Sergeant Dennis Becker: Joe Santos
Evelyn "Angel" Martin : Stuart Margolin
Beth Davenport: Gretchen Corbett

BROADCAST HISTORY
Sept. 1974-May 1977 — Friday, 9-10 p.m.
June 1977 — Friday, 8:30-9:30 p.m.
July 1977-Jan. 1979 — Friday, 9-10 p.m.
Feb. 1979-March 1979 — Saturday, 10-11 p.m.
April 1979-Dec. 1979 — Friday, 9-10 p.m.
March 1980-April 1980 — Thursday, 10-11 p.m.
June 1980-July 1980 — Friday, 9-10 p.m.

CHAPTER TWELVE:

THE EPISODES: FIRST SEASON

The Kirkoff Case

First telecast: Sept. 13, 1974.

Director: Lou Antonio. Writer: Stephen J. Cannell (from John Thomas James' story).

Regulars cast: Garner, Beery, Santos.

Guest cast: Julie Sommars (Tawnia), James Woods (Larry Kirkoff), Roger Davis (Travis Buckman), Philip Kenneally (Muggy Vinette), Abe Vigoda (Al Dancer), Dennis McCarthy (Calvin Carras), Milt Kogan (Marsh), Sandra deBruin (hostess), Dino Seragusa (maitre d'), Fred Lerner (parking attendant), Melissa Mahoney (carhop).

Though police have closed the case as unsolved, Larry Kirkoff, heir to a family fortune, still is considered the leading suspect in the murder of his parents. Kirkoff hires Rockford for a $20,000 fee to clear his name. Rockford has qualms about accepting the case because if the trail leads to his client, he could be out the fat paycheck. His investigation, however, soon points to two other suspects: Tawnia, the late Kirkoff's mistress, and Travis, a cowboy believed to have been Mrs. Kirkoff's paramour.

(Note: John Thomas James is the pen name of Roy Huggins. James Woods later would co-star with Garner in *Promise*, a 1986 made-for-TV movie that won five Emmys, including best-actor honors for Woods. Watch for Luis Delgado in a bit part, as a member of a wedding scene. In it, a justice of the peace can be heard calling Delgado by his own name. Delgado was a rarely noticed Rockford regular: He had been Garner's stand-in since the star's Maverick days.

The Dark and Bloody Ground

First telecast: Sept. 20, 1974.

Director: Michael Schultz. Writer: Juanita Bartlett (from John Thomas James' story).

Regular cast: Garner, Corbett, Beery, Santos.

Guest cast: Patricia Smith (Ann Calhoun), Nancy Malone (Elizabeth Gorman), Walter Brooke (Clyde Russell), Linden Chiles (Elliot Malcolm), Tom Bower (Officer Hensley), Matt Alaimo (Farber), Luis Delgado (police officer).

When Beth talks Rockford into helping an impoverished woman accused of murdering her screenwriter husband, Rockford himself becomes the target of would-be assassins. While trying to clear Beth's client, Ann Calhoun, Rockford is nearly run over by a truck, the first in a series of attempts on his life.

(Note: This is the first episode in which Beth Davenport, played by Gretchen Corbett, appears.)

The Countess

First telecast: Sept. 27, 1974.

Director: Russ Mayberry. Writer: Stephen J. Cannell (from John

Thomas James' story).

Regular cast: Garner, Santos, Corbett.

Guest cast: Susan Strasberg (Deborah), Dick Gautier (Carl Brego), Art Lund (Mike Ryder), Tom Atkins (Lieutenant Diel), Harold J. Stone (Sorrell), James Cromwell (Terry), Todd Martin (policeman), Florence Lake (old woman).

Rockford is hired to discourage the blackmailer of a wealthy Texan's socialite wife. Seems "the Countess," as she's commonly known, jumped bail on a minor criminal charge years earlier. Rockford tries to convince her to tell all to her husband and the police, but she fears the disclosure will ruin her elegant lifestyle. And though her troubles disappear when the extortionist is found fatally shot, Rockford's are only beginning. Police consider him a leading suspect.

(Note: Tom Atkins would return in other episodes during the first two seasons in the recurring role of Lieutenant Diel. He was Sergeant Becker's superior and often Rockford's foil. He is perhaps best known for roles in films such as *The Fog, Halloween III: Season of the Witch* and *Lethal Weapon*.)

Exit Prentiss Carr

First telecast: Oct. 4, 1974

Director: Alex Grasshoff. Writer: Juanita Bartlett (from John Thomas James's story).

Regular cast: Garner, Beery.

Guest cast: Corinne Camacho Michaels (Janet Carr), Mills Watson (Larsen), Warren Kemmerling (Furlong), Stephen McNally (Chief Bailey), Wallace Rooney (Eric Saunders), William Jordan (Terry Warde), Roberta Collins (Nancy Heldman), Hand Rolike (Eddie), Thomas Ruben (delivery boy).

When Rockford is hired to check on the whereabouts of a philandering husband, Prentiss Carr, he finds the man murdered in his Bay City hotel room. But when he tells local police and they go investigate, every shred of evidence points to suicide. Rockford first suspects the two detectives who investigated the scene doctored the evidence, and he isn't entirely convinced that Carr's widow, Janet, has nothing to do with the crime. But further prodding uncovers a blackmail operation.

Tall Woman in Red Wagon

First telecast: Oct. 11, 1974

Director: Jerry London. Writer: Stephen J. Cannell (from John Thomas James's story).

Regular cast: Garner, Beery.

Guest cast: Sian Barbara Allen (Sandra), George DiCenzo (Stoner), Angus Duncan (Joe Baron Jr.), Susan Damante (Charlotte Duskey), John Crawford (Dr. Kenilworth), Dave Morick (James Darrow), Ryan MacDonald (hotel manager), Rudy Diaz (Matty).

Rockford turns to grave robbery when he is hired to investigate the disappearance of a statuesque beauty who cleared out in her red station wagon. The trail uncovers an underworld connection and leads to a cemetery, a pullman car and the office of a strange doctor. Rockford is hampered, meanwhile, by the amateurish deductions of his client, the mission woman's newspaper co-worker and an IRS agent.

The Case is Closed

First telecast: Oct. 18, 1974 (90-minute episode).

Director: Bernard L. Kowalski. Writer: Stephen J. Cannell (from John Thomas James' story).

Regular cast: Garner, Beery.

Guest cast: Joseph Cotten (Warner Jameson), Sharon Gless (Susan Jameson), James McEachin (David Shore), Eddie Fontaine (Lieutenant Larry Pierson), Joseph Della Sorte (Torrance Beck), Fred Sadoff (Howard Kasanjian), Jude Farese (Harry), Del Monroe (Vic), Norman Bartold (Hollis Cotton), Stu Nesbit (bartender), Geoffrey Land (Mark).

Warner Jameson suspects his prospective son-in-law is a phony and hires Rockford to investigate the young man's past. After a rough trip to Newark, N.J., and harassment from both mobsters and federal agents, Rockford would like to quit. He has been trailed, threatened, beaten up and kidnapped because he uncovered an underworld connection. But circumstances won't permit it and he learns that Jameson will go to grave extremes to protect his daughter.

The Big Ripoff

First Telecast: Oct. 25, 1974.

Director: Vincent McEvesty. Writer: Jo Swerling Jr. (from John Thomas James' story).

Regular cast: Garner, Beery.

Guest cast: Jill Clayburgh (Marilyn Polonski), Nedra Deen (Nancy Frazer), Normann Burton (Melvyn Moss), Fred Beir (Steve Nelson), Kelly Thordsen (sheriff), Warren Vander (Pitt), Suzanne Somers (Ginny).

Rockford hopes to make a huge recovery fee by locating a supposedly dead man who swindled an insurance company out of $400,000, but the insurance company won't listen to his evidence. Rockford was hired by Nancy Frazer to find out if her lover, Steve Nelson, died accidentally or was done in by his wife, who "miraculously" survived a plane crash. But when he turns up evidence that the man may be alive, Nancy suddenly drops out of sight—without paying Rockford, naturally. The trail, then, leads to an art colony where model Marilyn Polonski not only helps Rockford, but nurses him after attacks by his adversaries.

(Note: Suzanne Somers, three years from becoming a pop celebrity in *Three's Company*, has one lineless scene—but you can't miss her. In the sequence, which opens the show, Rockford puts his underhanded sharps on display. Attempting to meet her—in the line of duty, mind you—he parks rented cars on either side of her automobile, so close she can't open the doors to her vehicle. Then it's Rockford to the rescue.)

Find Me If You Can

First telecast: Nov. 1, 1974.

Director: Lawrence Doheny. Writer: Juanita Bartlett (from John Thomas James' story).

Regular cast: Garner, Beery, Santos.

Guest cast: Joan Van Ark (Barbara Kelbaker), Paul Michael Glaser (Ralph Correll), Jean Allison (Mrs. Kelbaker), James Lydon (Wyatt), Tony Eppen (Broder), Richard Brout Miller (Sergeant Doane), Joseph Stern (Morgan Tallman), Adrian Ricard (Miss Conner).

An unusual case for Rockford. A secretive young woman who won't reveal her identity hires him to find someone. "Who do you want me to find?" asks Rockford. "Me," she answers. Though Rockford soon discovers his client is Barbara Kelbaker, a small town girl with an independent mind, she neglects to tell him that her real purpose is to hide from Denver's underworld leader, Ralph Correll. Seems she ran off with a bundle of her mob-boss boyfriend's money—and is using Rockford to make sure her tracks are covered.

In Pursuit of Carol Thorne

First telecast: Nov. 8, 1974.

Director: Charles S. Dubin. Writer: Stephen J. Cannell (from John Thomas James' story).

Regular cast: Garner.

Guest cast: Lynette Mettey (Carol Thorne), Robert Symonds (Miles), Jim Antonio (Cliff Hoad), Bill Fletcher (Nate Spinella), Irene Tedrow (Mrs. Hoad), Sandy Ward, (Detective Boris Sausman), Vince Howard (patrolman).

Rockford is hired to trail a young beauty just released from prison in the hope she will lead to the recovery of $1 million taken in a robbery three years earlier. Picking up Carol's trail at the prison gate, Rockford soon learns that his employer, Miles, is banking on Carol leading to Cliff Hoad, an accomplice in the robbery who escaped with the loot. Miles' theory is correct, but finding the money, even with Hoad's help, has drawbacks.

(Note: Jockey Laffit Pincay Jr. plays himself in a cameo role. Lou Antonio here becomes the first of many to have acted in and directed Rockford episodes. Others to hold both credits: Stuart Margolin, James Garner, Jackie Cooper and Dana Elcar).

The Dexter Crisis

First telecast: Nov. 15, 1974

Director: Alex Grasshoff. Writer: Gloryette Clark.

Regular cast: Garner.

Guest cast: Linda Kelsey (Louise), Lee Purcell (Susan), Tim O'Connor (Dexter), Rod Soble (Kermit Higby), Joyce Jameson (Marge White), Burke Byrnes (deputy sheriff), Bing Russell (Lieutenant).

Rockford is hired to search for a tycoon's mistress, Susan, who is missing from her apartment. After getting important information from the missing girl's roommate, a female law student named Louise, he is saddled with her "partnership" as the two follow a trail to Las Vegas. Susan is spotted, but the assignment is complicated by a second private detective, Higby, who seems to be following the same trail.

Caledonia, It's Worth a Fortune?

First telecast: Dec. 6, 1974.

Director: Stuart Margolin. Writer: Juanita Bartlett (from John Thomas James' story).

Regular cast: Garner.

Guest cast: Shelley Fabares (Jolene Hyland), Richard Schaal (Leonard Blair), William Traylor (Wilson), Sid Haig (B.J.), Ramon Bieri (Sheriff Prouty), Don Eitner (Gerald Hyland), Rudy Challenger (Dr. Watkins), Robert Ginty (Gib Moore), Robert Ellenstein (motel manager).

A deathly ill convict offers his wife a cryptic clue to the location of a $500,000 cache, hidden somewhere on a sprawling ranch in the rural community of Caledonia, and she hires Rockford to find it. Rockford, in turn, finds obstacles on both sides of the law. Though Rockford and his client, Jolene Hyland, have half the puzzle, Hyland's ex-con partner, Len, and Caledonia Sheriff Prouty hold the key to the second part.

(Note: Stuart Margolin, now an accomplished television director, cut his teeth as a director with this episode.)

Profit and Loss

First telecast: Dec. 20 and Dec. 27, 1974 (two-part episode).

Director: Lawrence Doheny. Writer: Stephen J. Cannell (from John Thomas James' story).

Regular cast: Garner, Beery, Corbett.

Guest cast: Ned Beatty (Fielder), John Carter (Alec Morris), Sharon Spelman (Doris Parker), Michael Lerner (Arnold Love), Val Bisoglio (Carl Bovino), Priscilla Pointer (Helen Morris), Paul Jenkins (Gorrick), Ray Giardin (Ted), Tom Rosqui (Norm Mitchell), Albert Paulen (Kurt), Al Stevenson (L.J.), Barry Cahill (sergeant).

A conglomerate's terrified computer programmer tries to hire Rockford, but kidnappers knock out Rockford and abduct his would- be client before he can explain the cause of his anxiety. When Rockford investigates the corporate leviathan, Financial Dynamics Inc., Fielder, head of the corporation, warns Rockford that the "kidnapping" of his top aide never occurred and for Rockford to quit prying. Rockford's interest heightens, however, when Doris Parker hires him to investigate the "accidental" death of her husband, a former FDI executive. Searching for clues that will link a stock-market scandal to the deaths of Doris' husband and an obscure printer, Rockford and Doris burglarize a print shop. Their print shop caper not only draws police, but reveals the ugly side of Fielder.

Aura Lee, Farewell

First telecast: Jan. 3, 1976.

Director: Jackie Cooper. Writer: Edward J. Lakso (from John Thomas James' story).

Regular cast: Garner.

Guest cast: Lindsay Wagner (Sara Butler), Robert Webber (Senator Evan Murdock), Greg Mullavey (Dirk Schaffer), Melissa Greene (Aura Lee), Henry Slate (Oscar), Bill Mumy (Trask), Linda Dano (Ellen Murdock).

When a new girl in town is found dead in her apartment from a heroin overdose, her only friend, Sara, insists she never used drugs and hires Rockford to prove it was murder. Rockford's investigation reveals that Senator Murdock gave the victim a lift in his car shortly before she was found dead. He also finds a con man had befriended Aura Lee.

THE ROCKFORD PHILE

(Note: Lindsay Wagner reprises character she first played in **The Rockford Files** pilot. Bill Mumy, who also appeared in the pilot, plays a different character here. The news commentator is played by NBC newswoman Kelly Lange.)

Sleight of Hand

First telecast: Jan. 17, 1975.

Director: William Wiard. Writers: Stephen J. Cannell and Jo Swerling (from Howard Browne's story).

Regular cast: Garner, Beery, Santos.

Guest cast: Tom Atkins (Lieutenant Diel), Lara Parker (Diana Lewis), Allan Miller (Michael Cordeen), Pat Delaney (Karen Mills), John Steadman (Morris Blauner), Gerald McRaney (Irv), Howard Curtis (Vincent Minnette), Wayne Wynne (Detective Olson).

Rockford searches for his girlfriend, Karen, whose sudden disappearance after a date coincides with the murder of her next- door neighbor. Rockford's prodding connects the incidents to a fugitive syndicate boss and his singer girlfriend.

Counter Gambit

First telecast: Jan. 17, 1975.

Director: Jackie Cooper. Writers: Howard Berk and Juanita Bartlett.

Regular cast: Garner, Beery, Santos, Margolin.

Guest cast: Eddie Fontaine (Moss Williams), Burr DeBenning (Harry Crown), Mary Frann (Valerie Thomas), Ford Rainey (Manny Tolan), M. Emmet Walsh (Edgar Burch), Garry Walberg (Arnold Cutter), Eric Server (Daniel Kramer), Barbara Collentine (Miss Bolting).

Just before being paroled, hot-tempered convict Moss Williams hires Rockford to find his missing girlfriend, Valerie. He neglects to mention, however, that he's really after a stolen pearl necklace in her possession. Rockford finds the girl and the jewelry but needs help from his former prison buddy, Angel, to outsmart Williams and his partner, Harry Crown.

(Note: This episode contains one of Rockford's finest scams, an ingenious method of safe cracking. Having befriended Valerie Thomas, the woman he knows to have a stolen diamond, he asks her to lock away temporarily a box he says contains valuables. It really contains a tape recorder, which he left on. Later she retrieves the box for him and Rockford need only count the clicks when playing back the recording to figure out the combination. The scheme works like a dream except for the fact that Rockford winds up wanted for grand theft. The episode also is Angel's first appearance since the movie pilot.)

Claire

First telecast: Jan. 31, 1975.

Director: William Wiard. Writers: Edward J. Lakso and Stephen J. Cannell.

Regular cast: Garner, Beery, Santos.

Guest cast: Linda Evans (Claire Prescott), Jackie Cooper (Captain Highland), Lane Smith (Willett), W.L. LeGault (Stone), M.P. Murphy (bartender), Douglas V. Fowley (Ted).

A former girlfriend, Claire Prescott, persuades Rockford to check on a friend under the pretense she is being victimized by a loan shark. The so-called friend turns out to be a missing narcotics officer. Rockford finds himself on the wrong side of both police and a pair of mobsters who kidnap Rocky, believing Rockford holds the key to the missing officer and Claire's underworld connection.

Say Goodbye to Jennifer

First telecast: Feb. 7, 1975.

Director: Jackie Cooper. Writers: Juanita Bartlett and Rudolph Borchert.

Regular cast: Garner, Beery, Santos.

Guest cast: Hector Elizondo (John Micelli), Thayer David (Carl Birrell), Pamela Hensley (Jennifer Rayburn), Regis J. Cordic (Dr. Stuart), Kate Woodville (Marilyn Rae), Ken Swofford (Floyd Ross), Len Lesser (Colby).

A photographer, John Micelli, hires Rockford to find a fashion model who is suspected of murder. Micelli is convinced that Jennifer is still alive—somewhere in Seattle—even after Rockford turns up dental records indicating she burned to death in a flaming auto accident. He asks Rockford, an old friend, to find her. When the dentist is worked over by hoodlums, Rockford also becomes convinced Jennifer is alive.

Charlie Harris at Large

First telecast: Feb. 14, 1975.

Director: Russ Mayberry. Writer: Jekial Marko (from John Thomas James' story).

Regular cast: Garner, Beery, Santos, Corbett.

Guest cast: Tony Musante (Charlie Harris), Diana Muldaur (Linda Bannister), David Spielberg (Sergeant Tom Garvey), Warner Anderson (Arthur Bannister), Zekial Marko (Dr. Gabriel), Mel Stuart (police lieutenant), Eddie Firestone (Haines).

Charlie Harris, Rockford's former prison cellmate, now a playboy, becomes the leading suspect in the murder of his wealthy wife. He begs Rockford to find the one person who can clear him, a woman with whom he had an affair, but doesn't know the woman's name or where she can be found. Rockford finds Charlie's story difficult to swallow, until the woman's photo appears on a newspaper society page with her aging but rich husband. Rockford's efforts to track her down are hampered by both her unsavory husband and police, led by Sergeant Garvey, who would like to lock up Rockford and Charlie and throw away the key.

(Note: During the 1973-74 season, Tony Musante starred as Detective David Toma in *Toma*, the series for which Jim Rockford's character was created. The episode that would have featured Rockford, however, never appeared on *Toma*. Writer Zekial Marko does double duty here, appearing as Dr. Gabriel. David Spielberg makes his first of two appearances as Sergeant Tom Garvey.)

The Four Pound Brick

First telecast: Feb. 21, 1975.

Director: Lawrence Doheny. Writers: Leigh Brackett and Juanita Bartlett.

Regular cast: Garner, Beery, Santos, Margolin.

Guest cast: Edith Atwater (Kate Banning), Paul Carr (Sergeant Andrew Wilson), Tom Atkins (Lieutenant Diel), Jess Walton (Laura Smith), Wyatt Johnson (Officer Curson), William Watson (Ross), John Quade (Tenner), Jack Knight (Officer Drexel), Bruce Tuthill (Walter), John Furlong (minister).

When police write off a rookie's death as accidental, Rockford is hired by his father, Rocky, and the mother of the dead officer, Kate Banning, an old family friend. She is convinced her son was not involved in a traffic mishap. Rockford soon agrees, finding the dead man's partner, Sergeant Wilson, is meeting secretly with gangsters. The investigation, naturally, puts Rockford on the wrong side with both police and the mob.

Just By Accident

First telecast: Feb. 28, 1975

Director: Jerry London. Writers: Charles Sailor and Eric Kaldor.

Regular cast: Garner, Beery, Santos, Margolin.

Guest cast: David Spielberg, (Sergeant Garvey), Neva Patterson (Louise Hartman), Fred Sadoff (Matt Springfield), E.J. Peaker (Jeannie Szymczyk), Oliver Clark (K. Julian Krumb), Steven Keats (Duane Bailey), Joey Aresco (Billy Jo Hartman), Millie Slavin (bank officer), Susan Keller (Vivian).

A mother hires Rockford to investigate the death of her estranged son, a demolition-derby driver whose car plunged off a cliff, an incident police have termed an accident. Rockford must answer how the son was able to afford a $200,000 policy on his life and soon uncovers a clever insurance-claim racket. When a contingent beneficiary, Jennie Szymczyk, leads Rockford to executive Matt Springfield, who masterminded the scam, Springfield sics his henchman on the detective, plotting another "accident."

(Note: This episode reunited Neva Patterson and James Garner, who co-starred in Garner's previous series, *Nichols*. Patterson played Ma Ketchum, matriarch of the notorious Ketchum family, Nichols' prim adversary throughout the 1971-72 series. Patterson and Noah Beery, meanwhile, once co-starred in *Doc Elliot*.)

Roundabout

First telecast: March 7, 1975.

Director: Lou Antonio. Writers: Mitchell Lindemann and Edward J. Lakso.

Regular cast: Garner.

Guest cast: Jesse Welles (Nancy Wade), Mills Watson (Edward Moss), Ron Rifkin (Tom Robertson), Frank Michael Liu (Kenneth Mamato), George Wyner (Strock), Virginia Gregg (Eleanor), Joe E. Tato (Agent Hanzer), Fred Lerner (Freeman), Chuck Hicks (Klaus).

Rockford travels to Las Vegas to deliver an insurance check to a beautiful young recording artist, Nancy Wade, but discovers she's a prisoner of a syndicate that's exploiting her. Rockford's problems begin when he finds Nancy in a dingy hotel room, where syndicate hoodlums assault him and steal the $10,000 check. With help from a Japanese investor also being victimized by the underworld group, Rockford sets out to track down the brains of the operation.

James Garner as "The Castaway Cowboy"
on THE WONDERFUL WORLD OF DISNEY.

CHAPTER THIRTEEN:

THE EPISODES: SECOND SEASON

James Garner and Noah Berry

The Aaron Ironwood School of Success

First telecast: Sept. 12, 1975.

Director: Lou Antonio. Writer: Stephen J. Cannell.

Regular cast: Garner, Beery, Santos, Margolin, Corbett.

Guest cast: James Hampton (Aaron Ironwood), Jerome Guardino (Vito), Ken Swofford (Federal Agent Patrick), Jonathon Lippe (Nino).

Rockford's instincts as an ex-con and a private investigator lead him to suspect a friend's motives when Aaron Ironwood, who lived with the Rockfords as a child, begs for an unusual favor. He wants to sign his multi-million-dollar firm over to Rockford to protect it from mobsters. The truth: Rockford's being scammed. Ironwood's School of Success is merely a old-fashioned pyramid scheme, and it's a toss-up who poses the bigger danger, mobsters or the federal government.

The Farnsworth Stratagem

First telecast: Sept. 19, 1975.

Director: Lawrence Doheny. Writer: Juanita Bartlett.

Regular cast: Garner, Beery, Santos, Margolin, Corbett.

Guest cast: Linda Evans (Audrey), Pat Finley (Peggy Becker), John Crawford (Christian), Paul Jenkins (Simon Lloyd), H.M. Wynant (Danzil), Al Hansen (Guardrell), Stephen Parr (Stuart).

Rockford goes to the aid of an unlikely victim of fraud, one-time bunco-cop Dennis Becker, who invested his money in a share of a condominium, only to find he owns only part of the hotel lobby. Also scammed was a young writer named Audrey. When Becker asks for help in getting their money back, Rockford, using jackhammers and an oil rig, recruits the help of Rocky and Angel and masterminds a scheme of his own to settle the score with the con artists.

(Note: Pat Finley makes his first of several appearances as Becker's wife, Peggy. Finley is perhaps best remembered for her role on *The Bob Newhart Show* as Ellen Hartley, sister to Newhart's Bob Hartley.)

Gearjammers

First telecast: Sept. 26 and Oct. 3, 1975 (two-part episode).

Director: William Wiard. Writer: Don Carlos Dunaway (from Stephen J. Cannell's story).

Regular cast: Garner, Beery, Santos.

Guest cast: Ted Gehring (Johnny LoSalvo), Scott Brady (Hammel), Rosemary DeCamp (Mary Ramsey), Bobby Hoy (Scheib), Al Stevenson (L.J.), Charles Cooper (Jack), Jack Kruschen (Koenig), Joe E. Tata (Willie), Bucklind Beery (Detective Mazurski), Terry Leonard (John Smith), Reb Brown (lifeguard).

Rocky has become the target of assassins and Rockford must find out why. It seems that, while selling tickets to a truckers' ball, Rocky unwittingly witnessed the prelude to a truck hijacking and an underworld pay-off. First, as Rockford searches for his father, he discovers that Rocky as been leading a "double life;" that he has a girlfriend named Mary Ramsey. Then, in his efforts to gather information about the criminals who already have made one attempt on Rocky's life, Rocky poses as a truck-company road boss.

(Note: Watch for Bucklind Beery in a small part as a rookie officer in part two. He is the son of Noah Beery.)

The Deep Blue Sleep

First telecast: Oct. 10, 1975.

Director: William Wiard. Writer: Juanita Bartlett (from Charles Floyd Johnson's story).

Regular cast: Garner, Beery, Corbett.

Guest cast: Janet MacLachlan (Adrienne Clarke), Robert Webber (Bob Coleman), Michael Conrad (George Macklan), Ric Mancini (Ray Porter), Melendy Britt (Millie), Robert B. Hays (Durren Weeks), Doria Cook (Margaux).

Rockford questions the heads of a fashion salon whose top model, Margaux, is found dead after placing a terrified phone call to her friend, Beth. Police have ruled the death either an accident or possible suicide. Rockford learns Margaux's boss, Adrienne Clarke, and an accountant, Bob Coleman, know more about the dead girl's affairs than they admit. The investigation uncovers Coleman's underworld connections and a trail of homicides through the studio.

The Great Blue Lake Land and Development Company

First telecast: Oct. 17, 1975.

Director: Lawrence Doheny. Writer: Juanita Bartlett.

Regular cast: Garner, Beery.

Guest cast: Dennis Patrick (Walter Hart), Richard B. Shull (Harry), Dana Elcar (sheriff), Mary Ann Chinn (Billie Carlton), Bartine Zane (Mildred), Bob Hastings (Paul Tanner).

When his car breaks down in Blue Lake, a small desert town, Rockford banks $10,000 in bail money for his client overnight in a real-estate company's safe. In the morning, the cash and attending salesman are gone. Rockford enlists the help of his father, Rocky, and an ex-con friend, Harry, in an attempt to recover the cash. Harry takes the job as salesman and Rocky poses as a prospective land buyer.

The Real Easy Red Dog

First telecast: Oct. 31, 1975.

Director: Ivan Dixon. Writer: Stephen J. Cannell.

Regular cast: Garner, Santos.

Guest cast: Stefanie Powers (Tina), Tom Atkins (Lieutenant Diel), Larry Cook (Dave), Wayne Grace (Deek), Nick Ferris (Pete Finch), George Wyner (Brice), Bruce Kirby Jr. (Friedler), Sherry Jackson (Jennifer).

Tina, a curiously evasive young woman, hires Rockford to investigate her sister's apparent suicide. It turns out to be a scam. Working to recover stolen jewels for an insurance company that does not want police intervention, Tina sold Rockford the phony suicide story to throw authorities off her trail. Rockford soon learns he's been had, a suicide turns out to be a homicide and he and Tina become the murder targets of racketeers.

Resurrection in Black and White

First telecast: Nov. 7, 1975.

Director: Russ Mayberry. Writers: Juanita Bartlett and Stephen J. Cannell.

Regular cast: Garner, Santos.

Guest cast: Joan Van Ark (Susan Alexander), William Prince (Arnold Newcomb), Sandra Smith (Shirley Atwater), Milton Selzer (Patrick Elber), John Lawler (Dave Kruger), John Danheim (Roy Pierce), Elven Howard (officer).

Susan Alexander, a beautiful magazine writer on the trail of a hot story, hires Rockford to help prove the innocence of Arnold Newcomb, who spent six years in prison for the murder of his girlfriend. With Susan tagging along, an initially skeptical Rockford discovers the supposed murder victim is alive and well—the perpetrator of an insurance scam that also involved a retired coroner. The pieces come together in a shoot-out at sea with Rockford pursuing in a speedboat covered by police helicopter.

Chicken Little's A Little Chicken

First telecast: Nov. 14, 1975.

Director: Lawrence Doheny. Writer: Stephen J. Cannell.

Regular cast: Garner, Beery, Santos, Margolin.

Guest cast: Ray Danton (Sierra), Frank Campanella (Frishette), Angelo Gnazzo (Joey Little), Sandy Ward (sheriff), Nicholas Worth (Kessler), Dave Cass (Sid), Kenneth Strange (Don), Charlie Horvath (Jose), Tom Williams (minister).

Angel asks Rockford to find Joey Little, who he claims disappeared owing him $2,000. Rockford discovers a $30,000 swindle is involved and, further, that mob-boss Sierra thinks Angel and Rockford are infringing on his territory. In a ploy designed to save their lives, Rockford stages a fake funeral for Angel.

(Note: Stuart Margolin singled out this episode as one of his favorite Rockfords.)

2 into 5.56 Won't Go

First telecast: Nov. 21, 1975.

Director: Jeannot Szwarc. Writer: Stephen J. Cannell.

Regular cast: Garner, Beery, Santos.

Guest cast: Mitchell Ryan (Colonel Hopkins), William Boyett (Sergeant Slate), Jesse Wells (Shana Bowie), Harvey Gold (Quentin Davis), Charles Napier (Billy Webster), Carol Vogel (Terry), John Kerry (Lieutenant Fenton), Eddie Firestone (Dwight Davis), Frank Maxwell (Colonel Bowie).

Rockford's old Army commander, Colonel Bowie, dies in a mysterious Jeep mishap officially called an accident. The man's daughter, Shana, suspects foul play and hires Rockford to investigate. The late colonel, coincidentally, called Rockford for help just before the accident and Rockford's phone number in Bowie's pocket initially made him a suspect. Despite resistance from Provost Marshal Hopkins, Rockford sets out to prove that Bowie's top sergeant, Slate, was responsible.

Pastoria Prime Pick

First telecast: Nov. 28, 1975.

Director: Lawrence Doheny. Writer: Gordon Dawson.

Regular cast: Garner, Beery, Corbett.

Guest cast: Kathie Browne (Mayor Karen Sanders), Richard Herd (Sheriff Gladish), Don Billett (Univaso), Bill Zuckert (Emmett Byrd), Bill Quinn (Judge Cline), Warren Kemmerling (Soper), William Lucking (Officer Kolodny), Smith Evans (Rita), Jack Garner (court clerk).

When his car breaks down in the peaceful little town of Pastoria while investigating a wife-and-child abandonment case, Rockford finds himself the victim of an intricately plotted frame. Rockford is first hit with an outrageous repair bill, followed by a set-up picture taken of him and the motel clerk, a teenage girl whose mother is mayor. Next comes a raid in which drugs are planted on him and Rockford soon finds himself behind bars. The charges: possession of narcotics for sale, transporting narcotics, grand theft auto, resisting arrest, destruction of private property, assault and battery, assaulting an officer of the law, attempted bribery, vandalism, reckless driving, contributing to the delinquency of a minor, and statutory rape. Even Rocky and Beth wind up in jail on trumped-up charges. With the help of a retired sheriff and the judge who heard his case, an on-the-lam Rockford sets out to clear his name and expose the blackmail ring, run by the mayor, district attorney and city police.

(Note: Watch for Jack Garner, brother of James Garner, in a bit part. Jack played other bit parts on *The Rockford Files* and later had a recurring role as LAPD Captain McEnroe during the series' last season.)

The Reincarnation of Angie

First telecast: Dec. 5, 1975.

Director: Jerry London. Writer: Stephen J. Cannell.

Regular cast: Garner, Beery.

Guest cast: Elayne Heilveil (Angie Perris), David Huddleston (Whitlaw), Wayne Tippit (Agent Dan Shore), Charles Siebert (Bettingen), Sharon Spelman (Susan), Eugene Peterson (Tom Perris), Jenny O'Hara (operator), Dick Durock (muscle).

Rockford aids a woman whose brother, a stock broker, mysteriously disappeared after giving her instructions to open a safe that turns out to contain $1 million in cash. The woman, Angie Perris, is convinced her brother was abducted from a phone booth by the underworld, but Rockford finds another possibility. It turns out he's not the only one looking for the stock broker. Federal agents also are on his trail, investigating the murder of an agent who had been working with Perris.

(Note: Wayne Tippit makes his first of several appearances as Federal Agent Dan Shore.)

The Girl in the Bay City Boy's Club

First telecast: Dec. 19, 1975.

Director: James Garner. Writer: Juanita Bartlett.

Regular cast: Garner, Margolin.

Guest cast: Blair Brown (Kate Flanders), Stewart Moss (Phelp/Deputy Kimball), Paul Stevens (George Welles), Joel Babiani (Thompkins), Chuck Hicks (Bell), William Bryant (Paul Flanders), Norman Bartold (Thatcher), Stacy Keach Sr. (Mosher).

While trying to find out if a high-stakes poker game is rigged, Rockford poses as a newspaper publisher and spends an evening of cards with Boys Club founder George Welles and other members. Later he is tailed home by Kate Flanders and learns that the man who supposedly hired him to do the job actually has been dead for two months.

(Note: This marks James Garner's only outing as director of a Rockford episode.)

The Hammer of C Block

First telecast: Jan. 9, 1976.

Director: Jerry London. Writer: Gordon Dawson.

Regular cast: Garner, Santos.

Guest cast: Isaac Hayes (Gandy Fitch), Lynn Hamilton (Eunice/Mrs. Bingham), Allan Rich ("Pebbles" Runkin), Annazette Chase (Debbie), James A. Watson Jr. (Arthur), Jack Somack (Oliver Prey), Bill Walker (Rosie), Helen Schustack (Betty), Hank Stohl (wino).

Gandolf Fitch, an ex-prison mate of Rockford, is released after serving 20 years for the murder of his wife, a crime he claims he didn't commit. He hires "Rockfish" to help find the true killer. Rockford, once a cellmate of Gandy, reluctantly accepts the case and the trail leads to a former hooker, now the respectable wife of a doctor. While the evidence indicates either Gandy or Eunice could have done it, the investigation takes a strange twist involving Eunice's stepchildren, Debbie and Arthur.

(Note: Isaac Hayes, a musician perhaps best known for his Oscar-winning score in the film, *Shaft*, makes his television dramatic acting debut as Gandy, his first of three Rockford appearances in that role. Stephen Cannell singled out this episode as being his favorite Rockford. Although he neither wrote nor directed the episode, he served as its on-line producer.)

The No-Cut Contract

First telecast: Jan. 16, 1976.

Director: Lou Antonio. Writer: Stephen J. Cannell.

Regular cast: Garner, Santos, Margolin, Corbett.

Guest cast: Rob Reiner (King Sturtevant), Dick Butkus (Dick Butkus), Wayne Tippit (Agent Dan Shore), Kathy Silva (Judy), Milt Kogan (first intruder), Mary Angela (Lisa).

Rockford becomes his own client in an attempt to discover why mobsters are after him, having linked him to a tape they want destroyed. It seems that King Sturtevant, a small-time pro quarterback was caught by federal agents and questioned about the tapes, bearing evidence against underworld figures. Sturtevant found Rockford's name in the phone book and told the officers that Rockford has them, siccing his troubles on the hapless P.I.

A Portrait of Elizabeth

First telecast: Jan. 23, 1976.

Director: Meta Rosenberg. Writer: Stephen J. Cannell.

Regular cast: Garner, Corbett, Santos.

Guest cast: John Saxon (Dave Delaroux), Robert Riesel (Mickey Silver), Wayne Tippit (Agent Dan Shore), Ned Wilson (Arnold Adams), Kate Woodville (Karen Silver), James Murtaugh (Tom Hanson), Cynthia Sykes (Susan Valero), Tom Atkins (Lieutenant Diel), Chuck Winters (Marley), Angus Duncan (Morley Dayton).

Jealous and suspicious, Rockford reluctantly agrees to look into some apparently shady financial dealings—the possible theft of cashier's checks—for Beth's suave new gentleman friend, Dave Delaroux. The case is soon complicated, however, when Beth is harassed by a psychotic admirer.

(Note: In this episode we finally learn there once was a romance between Rockford and Beth.)

Joey Blue Eyes

First telecast: Jan. 30, 1976.

Director: Lawrence Doheny. Writer: Walter Dallenbach.

Regular cast: Garner, Margolin, Corbett.

Guest cast: Michael Ansara (Joey), Suzanne Charney (Paulette), James Luisi (Striker), James Lydon (Barrow), Robert Yuro (Gannon), Eddie Fontaine (Sweet Tooth), Mickey Caruso (Shep), Normal Bartold (Evans), Sandy Kenyon (Mitchell).

Joey, an ex-con trying to go straight in the restaurant business, is being foreclosed by an unsavory group of corporate swindlers, who loaned him money at "shark" rates and, in addition, assaulted his daughter. With much difficulty, Rockford restrains Joey from physical action. Instead, Rockford recruits the aide of Beth and Angel, then finesses an elaborate scam to foil Joey's adversaries.

(Note: James Luisi was to return the following season in the recurring role of Lieutenant Doug Chapman, replacing Tom Atkins' character as Becker's superior and Rockford's primary foil.)

In Hazard

First telecast: Feb. 6, 1976.

Director: Jackie Cooper. Writer: Juanita Bartlett.

Regular cast: Garner, Beery, Santos, Corbett.

Guest cast: Joseph Campanella (Arnold Bailey), Frank Campanella (Marty Jordan), Richard Venture (Frank Metcalf), Skip Ward (Walt Rayner), Ben Frank (Howard Nystrom), Melendy Britt (Connie), Joe E. Tata (Solly Marshall), Linda Dano (Marie).

Beth needs Rockford's help after she counsels a stock broker in a tax suit and suddenly finds herself in jail and the target of an assassination attempt. While Beth is reluctant to reveal details about her clients, broker Arnold Bailey and union executive Frank Metcalf, she realizes their activities extend into the underworld and her life and others are threatened. Rockford finds her clients are involved in the theft of pension-fund money from a syndicate-controlled union.

The Italian Bird Fiasco

First telecast: Feb. 13, 1976.

Director: Jackie Cooper. Writer: Edward J. Lakso.

Regular cast: Garner, Santos.

Guest cast: William Daniels (Thomas Caine), Camilla Spary (Evelyn Stoneman), Ron Silver (Ted Haller), William Jordon (Jeffers), Peter Palmer (Stack), Eric Server (Whitlock), Gerald S. Peters (Edward Barrows), Dean Santoro (Collins), George Sawaya (Fricke), Ivor Barry (Cryder), Peter Ashton (clerk), D'Mitch Davis (guard).

After fulfilling a commission to purchase a valuable sculpted bird at an auction, posing as an art dealer, Rockford is attacked by mysterious assailants who break the sculpture into pieces and flee without explanation. Attempting to make sense of the incident, Rockford investigates and uncovers an international smuggling ring. Further, he suspects that a rival bidder, Evelyn Stoneman, may be involved.

Where's Houston?

First telecast: Feb. 20, 1976.

Director: Lawrence Doheny. Writer: Don Carlos Dunaway.

Regular cast: Garner, Beery, Santos, Corbett.

Guest cast: Lane Bradbury (Houston), Del Monroe (Charlie), Dabbs Greer (Pete Preli), Raymond O'Keefe (Hal), Murray MacLeod (Jerry), Robert Mandan (Blackthorn), Rodolfo Hoyos (Carlos), Bill Thornton (photographer).

One of Rocky's old cronies, Preli, hires Rockford to help his apparently-kidnapped granddaughter, Houston. The nature of Rockford's case changes dramatically when the granddaughter soon turns up unharmed—saying she had been on a geological trip to Mexico — and the grandfather turns up dead. Rockford's investigation uncovers a plot to buy up real estate, including Preli's property in a run-down part of town. The trail eventually leads to Houston's new friend, who is involved in real estate.

Foul on the First Play

First telecast: March 12, 1976.

Director: Lou Antonio. Writer: Stephen J. Cannell (from

Charles Floyd Johnson's story).

Regular cast: Garner.

Guest cast: Lou Gossett Jr. (Marcus Hayes), Dick Davaloe (Manny Stickells), David White (Martin Eastman), Pepper Martin (Greg Smith), Al Ruscio (Tom Corell), Chuck Bowman (Commissioner Treymayne), James Ingersoll (Sorenson), Vincent Cobb (Ray Fairchild), John Mahon (Todd Morris).

Rockford accepts an assignment from Marcus Hayes, thinking he is still a parole officer. Rockford discovers Hayes has become a private investigator (using the name Mark O'Brien) and is using him as a decoy to help a client obtain a new basketball franchise. Our hero puts his own game plan into motion.

(Note: This episode reunites Garner and Gossett, who co-starred in 1971's *Skin Game*. Gossett's character would return later in the series, teaming up with Gandy Fitch in the private detective business.)

A Bad Deal in the Valley

First telecast: March 19, 1976.

Director: Jerry London. Writers: Donald L. Gold and Lester William Burke.

Regular cast: Garner, Beery, Santos, Corbett.

Guest cast: Susan Strasberg (Karen Stiles), Russ McGinn (Fred Sutherland), Reg Parton (Jerry Sutherland), David Sabin (Murray Slauson), Rod Cameron (Jack Chilson), Veronica Hamel (Sandy Lederer), Jack Colvin (preacher), Gordon Jump (Appleby), John Lupton (Tony Lederer), Fritzi Burr (maid), Dudley Knight (real estate agent).

Karen Stiles, a former girlfriend, asks Rockford to deliver a briefcase, supposedly containing escrow papers, to another agent. Rockford winds up hip deep in trouble because the case really is stuffed with $100,000 in counterfeit money. Karen swears she was unaware the money was phony. She is kidnapped by assailants who haul her away in her own car.

James Garner plays a convicted murderer in THE ART OF LOVE, alongside Dick Van Dyke, Elke Sommer, Angie Dickinson and Ethel Merman.

GARNER'S OTHER ROLES

Rockford begins to fall for his client, Dr. Megan Dougherty (Kathryn Harrold), a blind psychologist who is being harassed by an unknown assailant.

CHAPTER FOURTEEN:

THE EPISODES: THIRD SEASON

The Fourth Man

First telecast: Sept. 24, 1976.

Director: William Wiard. Writer: Juanita Bartlett.

Regular cast: Garner, Beery, Santos, Margolin, Corbett.

Guest cast: Sharon Gless (Lori), John McMartin (Tim Farrell), Michael Bell (Stehler), Jack Garner (mailman), Candace Howerton (clerk), Dianne Harper (Susan).

Lori, a stewardess friend of Rockford, becomes the target of an assassin in an airport parking lot and Rockford soon discovers the prime suspect is a cold-blooded hit man. Lori's only clue to the attempt on her life was that passenger Tim Farrell overreacted to her friendly chit-chat that he was not a "regular" on the airline's passenger list. Farrell vehemently denied the "regular" charge. Soon after, attempts on Lori's life began. Farrell is easily tracked to his coin store, where Rockford, posing as a customer, uncovers leads to the man's other occupation as a gun for hire.

The Oracle Wore A Cashmere Suit

First telecast: Oct. 1, 1976.

Director: Russ Mayberry. Writer: David Chase.

Regular cast: Garner, Beery, Santos, Corbett.

Guest cast: Robert Webber (Clementi), Robert Walden (Silverstein), James Luisi (Lieutenant Chapman), Pepe Seona (Ochoa), James Hong (Kumago), Gary Epper (Larry), Ralph Garrett (Sal), John Furlong (detective), Terry O'Connor (Eileen).

A renowned psychic makes life uncomfortable for Rockford when he claims the P.I. knows more than he's letting on about the slaying of a dope dealer. Lieutenant Chapman is convinced that the psychic, Clementi, has supernatural powers and when he leads police along the beach to Rockford's mobile home, they want some answers from Rockford. Widespread publicity that always accompanies Clementi alerts the underworld to Rockford's possible involvement and they pay him an unfriendly visit. They think he has the $80,000 the dead man received for a cocaine delivery. Rockford, meanwhile, explores the possibility that Clementi is a phony.

The Family Hour

First telecast: Oct. 8, 1976.

Director: William Wiard. Writer: Gordon Dawson.

Regular cast: Garner, Beery, Santos, Margolin.

Guest cast: Kim Richards (Marin Ross Gaily), Burt Young (Stu Gaily), Ken Swofford (Al Jollett), Paul Koslo (Pittson), Marge Wakeley (Cecil Goss), Fred Lerner (Morabito), Adrian Ricard (receptionist), Janice Carroll (duty clerk).

The Rockfords, father and son, are about to embark on a fishing trip to Baja when a 9-year-old girl shows up outside Rockford's trailer. Rockford proceeds to look for her father, Stu Gaily, who is on the run from a double-dealing narcotics agent, Al Jollett, and the mob.

Feeding Frenzy

First telecast: Oct. 15, 1976.

Director: Russ Mayberry. Writer: Stephen J. Cannell (from Lester William Berke and Donald Gold's story).

Regular cast: Garner, Beery, Santos, Corbett.

Guest cast: Eddie Firestone (Charlie Blaylock), Susan Howard (Sandy Blaylock), Joseph Della Sorta (Lucy Carbone), Richard Le Pore (Lieutenant Dan Hall), Pepper Martin (Mickey Wanamaker), Luke Askew (Al), Tony Epper (Sherm).

Sandy Blaylock convinces Rockford that her father, Charlie, a reformed drunk, wants to make up for his larcenous past by returning $500,000 that he stole from an oil company three years earlier. Charlie stashed the money in a safe deposit vault until the statue of limitations ran out. Rockford soon discovers mobsters also are waiting for the statute to expire, figuring Charlie will lead them to the loot. Complications arise when the mobsters abduct Charlie's daughter.

Drought at Indianhead River

First telecast: Nov. 5, 1976.

Director: Lawrence Doheny. Writer: Stephen J. Cannell.

Regular cast: Garner, Beery, Santos, Margolin, Corbett.

Guest cast: Robert Loggia (Dominic Marcon), Vincent Baggetta (David), Rhonda Copland (Delores), Anthony Carbone (Brad), Nick Dimitri (Sammy).

To Rockford's dismay, Angel strikes it rich in real estate. The windfall turns out to be part of a tax swindle arranged by the mob. While Angel enjoys his new riches, Rockford learns the mob now wants Angel out of the way so it can collect its money. Rockford sets out to save Angel from two killers who have been hired to finish Angel.

Coulter City Wildcats

First telecast: Nov. 12, 1976.

Director: Russ Mayberry. Writer: Don Carlos Dunaway.

Regular cast: Garner, Beery, Corbett.

Guest cast: Dennis Burkley (Howard), John Anderson (O'Malley), Patricia Stich (Phyllis), Noble Willingham (Orzeck), Jerry Hardin (Link), Gordon Hurst (Willie), Norman Blankenship (Russ), Sharon Compton (Beehive), Terry Leonard (Ed), Don Nagel (driver).

Soon after Rocky is awarded a parcel of federal land in a public drawing, two toughs rough him up, demanding he sign away rights. When Rockford learns of the assault, he heads for the oil community of Coulter City to discover the reason for their interest in an unpromising oil lease.

So Help Me God

First telecast: Nov. 19, 1976.

Director: Jeannot Szwarc. Writer: Juanita Bartlett.

Regular cast: Garner, Beery, Corbett, Santos, Margolin.

Guest cast: William Daniels (Gary Bevins), Sandy Ward (Henshaw), Lieux Dressler (Margaret Raucher), Cliff Carnell (Gordy), Angelo Gnazzo (Pervis), Jason Wingreen (Foreman Rohrs), Robert Ray (Carl), John Lupton (Henry Franks), Jack Garner (bailiff), John B. Gowans (doctor).

Rockford is summoned before a grand jury investigating the alleged kidnapping of a union official. Before he is through testifying, he is cited for contempt and jailed indefinitely in federal prison when an aggressive U.S. attorney, Gary Bevins, convinces the grand jury that Rockford is withholding important information. The union leader is alleged to have talked to Rockford on the phone the day of his disappearance. When Rockford is released briefly on a technicality, he sets out to work up a defense.

(Note: Portions of the episode were filmed inside the federal prison at San Pedro, Calif.)

Rattlers' Class of '63

First telecast: Nov. 26, 1976.

Director: Meta Rosenberg. Writer: David Chase.

Regular cast: Garner, Beery, Margolin, Santos, Corbett.

Guest cast: Avery Schreiber (Azie), Elayne Heilveil (Regine Boyajian), John Durren (Leo Kale), James Wainwright (Gene Chechik), James Luisi (Lieutenant Chapman), Rudy Ramos (Bobby), Stacy Keach Sr. (Reverend), Sandra Kerns (Robin), Ed Vasgersian (Hank), Stanley Brock (Elliot Deutch).

Angel's getting married and Rockford's his best man. Well, not really. Angel's merely running a scam to swindle an Armenian family in a real estate deal. Rockford's an unwitting accomplice. Shortly after the wedding, Rockford discovers he has been used by Angel, who passed himself off as a Canadian beer baron seeking to buy the Armenian family's filled-in dump site. Seems something valuable is buried there. But now the vengeful Armenians intend to bury Angel and Rockford there as well.

(Note: Stuart Margolin singled out this episode as being one of his favorites.)

Return to the Thirty-Eighth Parallel

First telecast: Dec. 10, 1976.

Director: Bruce Kessler. Writer: Walter Dallenbach.

Regular cast: Garner, Beery, Santos.

Guest cast: Ned Beatty (Brennan), Michael Ebert (Nejman), Paul Stevens (Stabile), Veronica Hamel (Marcy), Normann Burton (Markel), Robert Karnes (Hulette), John Mahon (Lieutenant Hayes), Chuck Winters (Lindsay), Jeff David (Martin).

Brennan, an old Army buddy, shows up at Rockford's trailer claiming to have fallen on hard times. Co-incidentally, Marcy Brown arrives seeking Rockford's help in finding her sister. Before Rockford can turn her down, Brennen accepts the case. The search starts at the mansion of multi-millionaire Stabile and it soon is apparent that a 3,000-year-old Sang-Yin vase—not her sister—is the real object of Marcy's quest.

Piece Work

First telecast: Dec. 17, 1976.

Director: Lawrence Doheny. Writer: Juanita Bartlett.

Regular cast: Garner, Beery, Santos.

Guest cast: Michael Lerner (Murray Rosner), Harvey Vernon (Leedy), Ben Frank (Fred Molin), Jack Bannon (Deane), Simon Scott (McGill), Ned Wilson (Spiker), Michael Mancini (Pictaggi), Frank Maxwell (Lucas), James Luisi (Lieutenant Chapman).

Rockford is hired by an insurance company to check out an accident claim and stumbles onto a gun-running caper that makes him the target of both the underworld and federal agents. Starting the investigation at a swank health club, Rockford arouses the suspicions of member Murray Rosner, an apparent mob leader. Knowing Rosner is checking him out, Rockford reciprocates and discovers hidden machine guns. When he and Becker make a raid on the warehouse, however, they find federal agents also are on the case.

The Trouble with Warren

First telecast: Dec. 24, 1976.

Director: Christian I. Nyby II. Writer: Juanita Bartlett.

Regular cast: Garner, Beery, Santos, Corbett.

Guest cast: Ron Rifkin (Warren Weeks), Joe Maross (Lefcourt), Vince Howard (Kleinschmidt), Craig Chudy (Eunson), James Luisi (Lieutenant Chapman), Paul Jenkins (Hudson), Ann Randall (Catherine), Tom Bower (Cooperman).

Beth pressures Rockford into helping her brilliant cousin, suspected of murdering his boss. It becomes obvious to Rockford that Warren has been set up, and when the head of the firm is killed a short time later, Warren again is a suspect. Rockford doesn't like Warren and his contempt for Beth's cousin intensifies when his efforts to clear the man result in a litany of charges against Rockford. Among the charges: assault on a police officer, flight to avoid arrest, grand theft auto and malicious mischief. Rockford knows he's on the right track, though, when he learns that a U.S. Senate committee also is investigating the corporation's questionable business practices.

There's One In Every Port

First telecast: Jan. 7, 1977.

Director: Meta Rosenberg. Writer: Stephen J. Cannell.

Regular cast: Garner, Beery, Margolin.

Guest cast: Joan Van Ark (Christina Marks), Howard Duff (Eddie Marks), Michael Delano (Sharkey), John Machon (Victor Sherman), Steve Landesberg (Kenny Hollywood/Rhinehart), George Memmoli (Blast), Kenneth Tobey (Captain), John Dehner (Judge Lyman), Jack Riley (Adrian Lyman).

Christina Marks pleads with Rockford to use her $10,000 to play poker, hoping he can win enough to buy a kidney machine for her ailing father, Eddie. The poker party is cleaned out by masked bandits—a total take of $200,000—and Rockford suddenly realizes he was duped by Christina and Eddie, a father-daughter confidence team. When Rockford discovers they are currently in the middle of a bigger con involving the sale of a boat they don't own, he sets into motion a scheme of his own to settle the score.

Sticks and Stones May Break Your Bones, but Waterbury Will Bury You

First telecast: Jan. 14, 1977.

Director: Jerry London. Writer: David Chase.

Regular cast: Garner, Beery, Santos.

Guest cast: Simon Oakland (Vern St. Cloud), Cleavon Little (Billy Merrihew), George Pentecost (Colavito), Robert Riesel (Wass), Val Bisoglio (Marv), Katherine Charles (Susan Hanrahan), James Karen (La Pointe), Anthony Costello (Ted Clair), Linda Dano (Gwen Molinaro).

Rockford is hired by rival private investigators Vern St. Cloud and Billy Merrihew to track down the woman who has sabotaged their businesses, setting them up for felony raps that cost them their licenses. Rockford's probe reveals a conglomerate agency, Waterbury, is going to elaborate means to stamp out the competition, including the beating death of a third private investigator, Marv.

(Note: Simon Oakland makes his first of several appearances as Vern St. Cloud, scuzzball P.I.)

The Trees, the Bees and T.T. Flowers

First telecast: Jan. 21 and Jan. 28, 1977 (two-part episode).

Director: Jerry London. Writer: Gordon Dawson.

Regular cast: Garner, Beery, Santos, Corbett.

Guest cast: Strother Martin (T.T. Flowers), Karen Machon (Cathy Royale), Alex Rocco (Sherman Royale), Scott Brady (Meullard), Richard Venture (Dr. Crist), Fred Stuthman (Homer Hobson), Allen Williams (Dr. Fellows), Paul Sylvan (Steve Fisher), Jack Stauffer (Brubaker), Bob Hastings (Gidley), Roy Jenson (Winchell).

Before Rocky's eyes, his friend T.T. Flowers is spirited away from his three-acre farm in the valley by two white-coated men in a green van. When Rockford succumbs to Rocky's pleas to find his abducted friend, he uncovers a conspiracy in which a land developer has T.T.'s son-in-law in a bind and is forcing him to sell the old man's farm to him. That's why the son-in-law convinced his wife to have T.T. committed to a senior citizen's hospital, Horizon Crest. Rockford springs T.T. to give him a chance to disprove claims that he is senile and regain possession of his farm.

The Becker Connection

First telecast: Feb. 11, 1977.

Director: Reza S. Badiyi. Writer: Juanita Bartlett.

Regular cast: Garner, Santos, Beery, Margolin.

Guest cast: Jack Kelly (Alex Kasajian), Jack Carter (Marty Golden), Pat Finley (Peggy Becker), William Jordon (Officer Dolan), Bucklind Beery (Officer Mazurski), James Luisi (Lieutenant Chapman).

Becker is suspended on suspicions of dealing in drugs. He has been set up as the fall guy for a narcotics ring that has stolen a load of confiscated heroin from a police property room. When Rockford sets out to clear his friend's name, he discovers the theft was the work of a has-been comic (Marty Golden) and a nightclub owner (Alex Kasajian). Also in on the crooked deal is a cop, Officer Dolan, Becker's "best friend."

(Note: This episode reunites former *Maverick* co-stars Jim Garner and Jack Kelly. Kelly had played Bart Maverick, brother of Garner's Bret Maverick.)

Just Another Polish Wedding

First telecast: Feb. 18, 1977.

Director: William Wiard. Writer: Stephen J. Cannell.

Regular cast: Garner, Beery, Margolin.

Guest cast: Issac Hayes (Gandy Fitch), Louis Gossett Jr (Marcus Hayes), Pepper Martin (Mel), Anthony Charnota (Dancer), Walter Brooke (Gertmanian), Jack Collins (Finn Martin/Finn O'Herlihy), Barney McFadden (Fred Koska), Melendy Britt (Bride), Dennis Burkley (Bartender), George Skaff (Head waiter).

When Gandy Fitch, Rockford's one-time prison cellmate, tells Rockford he wants to get into detective work, Rockford steers him to parole officer-turned-P.I. Marcus Hayes. The two get together and Gandy inadvertently mentions to Hayes Rockford's effort to find a missing heir. That's when Hayes decides to go after the finder's fee himself.

New Life, Old Dragons

First telecast: Feb. 25, 1977.

Director: Jeannot Szwarc. Writer: David C. Taylor (from Bernard Rollins and Leroy Robinson's story).

Regular cast: Garner, Beery.

Guest cast: Irene Yah-Ling Sun (Mai), Kathleen Nolan (Cathy Hartman), Chris Napier (Donner), Charles Siebert (Gary Stillman), Luke Askew (Benson Kelly), Jim Ishida (Pham Vinh), Clyde Kusatsu (Nguyen), Al Stephenson (L.J.), James Callahan (Lew Hartman).

A young Vietnamese woman hires Rockford to locate her brother, a emigre who mysteriously disappeared after leaving a relocation center. The trail leads Rockford to a kidnapping plot involving three ex-soldiers, a CIA agent and $500,000 stolen from payrolls just before the fall of Saigon. Mai, working as a maid for engineer Lew Hartman and his wife, tells Rockford he was met instead by ex-G.I.'s Donner, Stillman and Kelly, kidnappers who think he has brought the half million to the U. S. from Vietnam. Hartman, who was a CIA agent in Vietnam, also thinks Mel's brother has the loot, but Rockford isn't convinced it's as simple as that.

To Serve and Protect

First telecast: March 11 and March 18, 1977 (two - part episode).

Director: William Wiard. Writer: David Chase.

Regular cast: Garner, Beery, Santos.

Guest cast: Joyce Van Patten (Lianne Sweeney), Jon Cypher (Michael Kelly), Leslie Charleson (Patsy Fossler), James Luisi (Lieutenant Chapman), Pat Finley (Peggy Becker), Luke Andreas (Sly), George Loros (Anthony Boy), Nick Dimitri (Dorsey).

A rich lawyer, Michael Kelly, hires Rockford to search for his fiancee and gives him an ultimatum: find her in 24 hours or he suffers fatal consequences. Rockford discovers that the woman, Patsy Fossler, has been marked for murder by the underworld. Rockford finds Patsy, but chooses to hide her until passage out of the country can be arranged. Complicating matters is the meddling of police groupie Lianne Sweeney, who double-crosses Becker, then blabs the whereabouts of Rockford's hiding place to the would-be killers.

(Note: Joyce Van Patten was the wife of Dennis Dugan, who later played Richie Brockelman.)

Crack Back

First telecast: March 25, 1977.

Director: Reza S. Badiyi. Writer: Juanita Bartlett.

Regular cast: Garner, Beery, Corbett, Santos.

Guest cast: Howard McGillin (Davey Woodhull), Joseph Mascolo (Gibby), Sondra Blake (Doreen), Conchata Farrell (Ella Mae White), John Calvin (Coach Preston Garnett), Bo Kaprall (Willie Gunther). Beth hires Rockford to find a missing witness who can provide an alibi for her client, a football player charged with homicide, when she is suddenly harassed by phone calls and pornographic gifts. Davey Woodhull, on trial in connection with the slaying of a bartender during a robbery, claims that at the time the crime was committed, he was on a date with Doreen, a married woman who does not want to get involved. During his search for Doreen, Rockford uncovers a link with the creep who is trying to break down Beth's courtroom performance.

Dirty Money, Black Light

First telecast: April 1, 1977.

Director: Stuart Margolin. Writer: David C. Taylor.

Regular cast: Garner, Beery, Santos, Margolin, Corbett.

Guest cast: John P. Ryan (Dearborn), Wesley Addy (Steiner), Roger Mosley (Larry), Joshua Bryant (Mike Wolf), Victor Argo (Judd Brown), John Chappell (Blake).

When Rocky returns home from a vacation in Hawaii, he finds huge sums of money arriving in the mail. When he also finds himself in Dutch with federal agents and the mob, it's up to Rockford to bail his father out of trouble. Rockford discovers that two racketeers had been scamming money from Las Vegas and using Rocky's address as a drop and pick-up port. Complicating matters is the fact that Angel stole a couple of bills and tried to break them.

Though attempts have been made on her life, Lori (Sharon Gless), a stewardess, enjoys a romantic interlude with her protector.

CHAPTER FIFTEEN:

THE EPISODES: FOURTH SEASON

Beamer's Last Case

First telecast: Sept. 16, 1977.

Director: Stephen J. Cannell. Writer: Stephen J. Cannell (from Booker Bradshaw and Calvin Kelly's story).

Regular cast: Garner, Beery, Santos.

Guest cast: Jack Kelly (Ralph Steel), James Whitmore Jr. (Fred Beamer), Bibi Besch (Monica Steel), Robert Loggia (Manny), Cal Bellini (Pedro Ramirez), Howard George (Phil Moreno), Phil Hoover (Dallas Walker).

Rockford investigates himself, in a sense. It seems that someone assumed Rockford's identity while he was vacationing and badly bungled a case, ran up huge expenses and antagonized clients who now want revenge. The trail leads to Rockford's nerdy mechanic, Fred Beamer, who has been living out fantasies of being a P.I. He bought numerous detective devices (using Rockford's credit cards), wrecked Rockford's car and cobbed a divorce investigation for Monica Steel, bringing the wrath of her husband down on an unwitting Rockford. Beamer's one saving grace? He accidentally was breaking up an underworld plot aimed at controlling the local taxicab business.

(Note: Despite the title, indicating this was his last case, James Whitmore Jr. was in fact making his first appearance in a recurring role as Fred Beamer, the "wannabe" detective. Garner's former *Maverick* co-star, Jack Kelly, marked his second Rockford appearance.)

Trouble in Chapter 17

First telecast: Sept. 23, 1977.

Director: William Wiard. Writer: Juanita Bartlett.

Regular cast: Garner, Beery, Santos.

Guest cast: Claudette Nevins (Ann Clement), Donna Baccala (Fran Avery), Tasha Martell (Marty Bach), Al Checco (Sam), Candace Howerton (Gloria).

An outspoken woman author, an anti-feminist whose best-selling book advocates traditional roles for women, hires Rockford to check out her suspicion that a feminist group has marked her for murder. Rockford soon learns she is not imagining things and that his own life is now in jeopardy. After one murder is committed, Rockford puts his life on the line to stop the assailant from striking a second time.

The Battle of Canoga Park

First telecast: Sept. 30, 1977.

Director: Ivan Dixon. Writer: Juanita Bartlett.

Regular cast: Garner, Beery, Santos, Corbett.

Guest cast: Nora Marlowe (Viola Wenke), Adrienne Marden (Lee Ronstadt), Tom Atkins (Lieutenant Diel), Elliott Street (Leonard Ronstadt), John Dennis Johnston (Hank).

Troubles mount for Rockford when his gun is stolen and used in the murder of a service station owner. Police don't believe him when he claims the weapon was taken from his cookie jar. Rockford draws up his own list of suspects, beginning with Viola Wenke, a cleaning women who had access to his trailer. After a series of dead ends, Rockford discovers that a dangerous para-military group is responsible when the group takes Rockford captive.

The Second Chance

First telecast: Oct. 14, 1977.

Director: Reza S. Badiyi. Writer: Gordon Dawson.

Regular cast: Garner, Margolin, Santos.

Guest cast: Isaac Hayes (Gandy Fitch), Dionne Warwick (Theda), Tony Burton (Joe Moran), Malachi Throne (Shapiro).

Gandy Fitch, now working as a bouncer at a third-rate bar, and Rockford team up again. Gandy asks for help in finding his girlfriend Theda, a nightclub singer who has been abducted by her brutal ex-husband, an paroled murderer. While conducting their investigation, Rockford and Gandy learn the Mafia has a special interest in Theda when they uncover a counterfeit poker chip scheme.

(Note: This episode, the third featuring Isaac Hayes as Gandy Fitch, contains a memorable scene: The only time that Gandy, grateful for Rockford's help, calls Rockford by his right name instead of "Rockfish.")

The Dog and Pony Show

First telecast: Oct. 21, 1977.

Director: Reza S. Badiyi. Writer: David Chase.

Regular cast: Garner, Beery, Santos, Margolin.

Guest cast: Joann Nail, (Mary Jo), George Loras (Tommy), Walter Brooke (Agent Sondman), Michael Bell (Krasny), Ed Lauter (Joey Bloomberg), Gary Crosby (Beau).

Rockford and Angel are ordered to join a psychiatric therapy group after Angel implicates Rockford in a petty theft. At one of the sessions, a frightened young woman, Mary Jo, a former mental patient, tells of receiving threats from the underworld. She insists the threats are real because of her friendship with Joey Bloomberg, a shady character who claims to be an intelligence man. When Rockford tries to determine whether she has legitimate reasons for thinking someone is following her, he runs afoul both the CIA and the Mafia.

Requiem for a Funny Box

First telecast: Nov. 4, 1977.

Director: William Wiard. Writer: James S. Crocker (from Burt Prelutsky's story).

Regular cast: Garner, Beery, Santos, Corbett.

Guest cast: Chuck McCann (Kenny Bell), Jodean Russo (Maxine), Meredith MacRae (Lori Thompson), Robert Quarry (Lee Russo), Jason Evers (Silvan).

A second-rate comic leaves Rockford dangling on a homicide charge rather than admit he has a joke file. Kenny Bell, the second banana of a now-separated comedy team, has Rockford deliver $10,000 to unknown burglars for the return of his "funny box." Instead of the jokes, however, Rockford finds the body of Lee Russo, the hot-tempered headliner who claimed Kenny stole his material. Rockford now must prove his innocence, but Kenny is no help, telling police that he "wouldn't think of owning a joke file."

Quickie Nirvana

First telecast: Nov. 11, 1977.

Director: Meta Rosenberg. Writer: David Chase.

Regular cast: Garner, Beery, Santos.

Guest cast: Valerie Curtin (Sky Aquarian), Kenneth Gillman (Alan Bayliss), James Luisi (Lieutenant Chapman), Quinn Redeker (Gordon Borcher), Dick Anthony Williams (Maceo).

Rockford does a favor for a girl camped in a makeshift pyramid outside his trailer, but the good deed gets him in Dutch with a man trying to cover up a homicide. Rockford allows a 40-year-old flower child, Sky Aquarian, to use his mailing address to avoid bill collectors, but thugs working for an attorney, Alan Bayliss, and his client, recording artist Maceo, find her. They accuse both her and Rockford of stealing $30,000 hush money Sky was to have delivered to a boardwalk blackmailer. It so happens a scamming phony guru is responsible, so Rockford and Sky go after him at the Gordon Borsher Sunshine Institute.

Irving the Explainer

First telecast: Nov. 18, 1977.

Director: James Coburn. Writer: David Chase.

Regular cast: Garner, Beery, Santos.

Guest cast: Barbara Babcock (Karen Hall), Roger Etienne (Major), Maurice Marsac (Giono), Paul Stewart (Buddy Richard), Irene Tsu (Daphne).

Karen Hall, a mysterious woman claiming to be a freelance writer, hires Rockford to do research work on the late director, Alvah Korper, and come up with biographical material. Rockford soon discovers that

Korper was a Nazi sympathizer and that two French secret police are also in Hollywood looking into the man's past. Turns out Karen duped Rockford, hoping his background check would help her find a valuable art treasure—a famous French painting by Watteau believed stolen by Nazis during World War II and sold to Korper. Rockford has no choice but to join her to protect both their lives from mysterious sources who also want the Watteau.

(Note: This episode reunites Garner and actor James Coburn, who served here as a director. They co-starred in *The Great Escape*, in 1963, and *The Americanization of Emily*, in 1964.

Hotel of Fear

First telecast: Nov. 25, 1977.

Director: Russ Mayberry. Writer: Juanita Bartlett.

Regular cast: Garner, Beery, Margolin, Santos.

Guest cast: Madison Arnold (Del Kane), James Luisi (Lieutenant Chapman), Vincent Baggetta (Murray), Eugene I. Peterson (Gagel), Frank De Kova (Nova), Stephen Coit (Welles), Barry Atwater (Roach).

Good food and posh quarters—with Lieutenant Chapman as his personal bodyguard—are part of the protective custody package the district attorney's office gives Angel to persuade him to testify against a notorious syndicate hit man. Angel makes the most of his good fortune—until the suspect is found not guilty. When mobster Del Kane is turned loose, Angel goes running to "Jimmy" for help.

Forced Retirement

First telecast: Dec 9, 1977.

Director: Alexander Singer. Writer: William R. Stratton.

Regular cast: Garner, Beery, Santos, Margolin, Corbett.

Guest cast: Margaret Impert (Susan Kenniston), Larry Hagman (Richard Lessing), Denny Miller (Chris Jencks), Ron Masak (Virgil Cheski).

Rockford investigates an underwater research project headed up by one of Beth's old college friends. Posing as a rich Oklahoman, he uncovers a scam involving the company's claim that it has developed a new offshore oil recovery device. Everything's going smoothly, in fact, until Angel meets Rockford in a restaurant with Susan Kenniston, a high official of the group, and blows Rockford's cover.

(Note: James Garner and Larry Hagman have shared a role. In the 1974 made-for-TV sequel to Garner's *Skin Game*, titled *Sidekicks*, Hagman took over the character originally played by Garner. Lou Gossett Jr., meanwhile, reprised his *Skin Game* role. Coincidentally, the sequel also starred Noah Beery.)

The Queen of Peru

First telecast: Dec. 16, 1977.

Director: Meta Rosenberg. Writer: David Chase.

Regular cast: Garner, Beery, Santos.

Guest cast: George Wyner (Kalifer), Ken Swofford (Carl Wronko), Susan Davis (Dot Wronko), Michael Morgan (Sean Wronko), Jennifer Marx (Shareen Wronko), Hunter von Leer (Skip), Christopher Gary (Ginger Townsend), James Luisi (Lieutenant Chapman), Paul Covonis (Donny Waugh), Joe E. Tata (Mike Trevino).

Rockford finds himself on the unlikely case of finding the family that stole his barbecue grill. It seems Rockford was hired by an insurance company to negotiate with criminals for the return of a $3 million stolen diamond. After making contact with mobsters, Rockford devises an exchange plan at the beach near his trailer. But before the plan is executed, the gem stashed in Rockford's barbecue is hauled off by a family from Peru, Ind., that is touring the Pacific coast in a camper. (They have no idea the rock is hidden in the ashes.) Now the search is on for the Wronko family.

(Note: Executive producer Meta Rosenberg, who directed, singled out this episode as being her favorite Rockford, "not just because I directed it,' she said, "but because it was a especially well-written story.")

The Deadly Maze

First telecast: Dec. 23, 1977.

Director: William Wiard. Writer: Juanita Bartlett.

Regular cast: Garner, Beery, Santos.

Guest cast: Larry Linville (Professor Von Albach), Corinne Michael (Tracy), J. Seven (George), John McKinney (Nick), Jack Collins (Victor), Cliff Carnell (Max), Ken Anderson (Todd).

Strapped for cash, Rockford takes a case he'd prefer to decline: his client's wife has disappeared and Rockford must find her. Rockford feels something isn't quite on the up and up, however. Turns out the client, Von Albach, an eccentric scientist, is putting Rockford through an elaborate stress test. Von Albach gives Rockford obscure clues about the missing Tracy, then observes his reactions under frustration. But one clue leads Rockford to a skid-row bar and discovery of Tracy's "other" lifestyle, which involves a homicide not anticipated by the erudite professor.

The Attractive Nuisance

First telecast: Jan. 6, 1978.

Director: Dana Elcar. Writer: Stephen J. Cannell.

Regular cast: Garner, Beery, Corbett.

Guest cast: Victor Jory (Ed LaSalle), Ken Lynch (Vince Whitehead), Dick Balduzzi (Don Silver), Joe Tornatore (Sid), John Morgan Evans (Vinnie), Joseph Dellasorte (Dave), Hunter von Leer (Skip).

Rocky goes into partnership with a stranger in a plan to open a roadside restaurant. But it seems a retired FBI agent is determined to get revenge on an old underworld figure, Vince Whitehead, Rocky's new business partner. When Eddie LaSalle shows up at the truck stop cafe, he assumes Rocky is also a mobster. Coming to his father's aid, Rockford must cope not only with the roughshod tactics of LaSalle, but fight off members of the underworld, from which Vince had not totally retired.

The Gang at Don's Drive - In

First telecast: Jan. 13, 1978

Director: Harry Falk. Writer: James S. Crocker.

Regular cast: Garner, Beery, Santos

Guest cast: Anthony Zerbe (Jack Skowron), Mills Watson (Stan Collier), Lawrence Casey (Bob Atcheson), Arlene Golonka (Jeanne Rosenthal), Elaine Princi (Jo Ann).

Jack Skowron, a washed up author, hires his old friend Rockford to research a high school class of 1962. In the process, Rockford comes across the cover-up of a homicide committed several years earlier. Skowron sends Rockford to the hometown of a girl who supposedly died of a ruptured appendix in 1961. He finds that her classmates, Stan Collier and Jeanne Rosenthal, now highly successful in business, were with the girl at the drive-in the night she died. Rockford's efforts to get their stories are thwarted by musclemen, who zero in on both him and Skowron.

The Paper Palace

First telecast: Jan. 20, 1978

Director: Richard Crenna. Writer: Juanita Bartlett.

Regular cast: Garner, Beery, Santos

Guest cast: Rita Moreno (Rita Capkovic), James Luisi (Lieutenant Chapman), Pat Finley (Peggy Becker), Bruce Kirby (Sid Loft), David Lewis (Burton Woodruff), Patricia Donahue (Eleanor Loft).

A prostitute, Rita Capkovic, hires Rockford to investigate mysterious death threats against her. After reluctantly agreeing to help Rita, Rockford quickly concedes her story is true when two French-speaking thugs nearly do him in while he is staked out at her apartment. The trail left by the suspects leads to a sophisticated businessman who hopes to prevent Rita from inheriting a fortune from his late partner.

(Note: Rita Moreno won an Emmy for this, her first of three appearances on Rockford. Moreno and Garner earlier co-starred in **Marlowe**, a 1969 motion picture in which Garner played private eye Phillip Marlowe.)

Dwarf in a Helium Hat

First telecast: Jan. 27, 1978

Director: Reza S. Badiyi. Writers: Stephen J. Cannell and David Chase.

Regular cast: Garner, Beery.

Guest cast: John Pleshette (Jay Rockfelt), Rebecca Balding (Carol Lansing), Gianni Russo (Gianni Tedesco), Milton Selzer (Irving Rockfelt), Rick Silvern (Edith Rockfelt), Ted Markland (Mel), Mary Nancy Brunett (Susan).

Rockford receives a death threat by telephone, but apparently it was intended for a flighty social parasite by the name of Jay Rockfelt, whose name appears ahead of Rockford's in the phone directory. Rockford sets out to warn Rockfelt of the impending danger. Rockford's good intentions fail to impress Rockfelt and his girlfriend, Carol Lansing, who are too involved in rock star Keith Stuart's Hollywood party. They finally realize their plight when Rockford saves them from kidnappers and death, using a chartered bus as a defense weapon in a touch-and-go chase.

South by Southwest

First telecast: Feb. 3, 1978

Director: William Wiard. Writer: Juanita Bartlett.

Regular cast: Garner.

Guest cast: Dorrie Kavanaugh (Christine van Deerlin), Carlos Romero (Agent Sam Gurolla), Don Chastain (Jon van Deerlin), Mark Roberts (Agent Kleinhoff), Jim Scott (Agent Ben Bast), Don Dubbins (Agent Frazee), Rob Clothworthy (Tommy).

Rockford is mistakenly abducted by federal agents and becomes involved in a plot to rescue an heiress from her husband, who is wheeling and dealing materials to less-than-friendly countries. Rockford is asked to contact international playgirl Christine van Deerlin on behalf of "national pride." Rockford's efforts to save Christine from her husband are further encouraged by the woman's apparent romantic interests in his welfare.

The Competitive Edge

First telecast: Feb. 10, 1978

Director: Harry Falk. Writer: Gordon Dawson.

Regular cast: Garner.

Guest cast: Stephen Elliott (Dr. Brinkman), Robert Hogan (Lester Shaw), Pepper Martin (Gustav), Jim McMullan (Perry Brauder), Neile McQueen (Joyce Brauder), George Murdock (Doc Holiday), John Lupton (Marty Sloan), John Fidoler (Bond), Dennis Fimple (Rhino), Sandie Newtown (Gail).

Rockford is hired to find an accused embezzler who jumped bail on a theft charge. Starting his investigation at banker Perry Brauder's health club, Rockford poses as a newsman. When his search for the missing banker gets too close to the truth, Dr. Brinkman has Rockford abducted and sent to an insane asylum out of state, where he is committed for "treatment" under a false name. Rockford's new priority, then, is to organize his fellow inmates in an explosive escape attempt.

The Prisoner of Rosemont Hall

First telecast: Feb. 17, 1978

Director: Ivan Dixon. Writer: Stephen J. Cannell (from Charles Floyd Johnson and Maryanne Rea's story).

Regular cast: Garner, Beery, Santos

Guest cast: Frances Lee McCain (Leslie Callahan), Kenneth Tobey (Max Kilmore), Buck Young (Jake Sand), Maurice Sherbanee (Kadahfi), Daniel Ades (Machmoud), Roc Carrott (Miller), Joyce Easton (Val).

Jake Sand, a college fraternity pledge, has been abducted by his brothers. He escapes and heads to Rockford's for help. Rockford isn't home and his brothers grab him again, leaving Jake's car by Rockford's trailer. Concerned, Rockford investigates the apparent kidnapping of his young friend, a promising journalism student. Though Rockford arrives on the campus incognito, his disguise is soon uncovered and he draws fire from the campus security chief, Max Kilmore. Rockford keeps at it, though. And with the help of journalism teacher Leslie Callahan and mysterious Arab agents, Rockford soon uncovers a lucrative kidnapping ring operating on campus—involving the campus police and the fraternity—and two murders, one of the victims being Jake.

The House on Willis Avenue

First telecast: Feb. 24,1978 (two - hour episode).

Director: Hy Averback. Writer: Stephen J. Cannell.

Regular cast: Garner, Beery, Santos.

Guest cast: Dennis Dugan (Richie Brockelman), Jackie Cooper (Garth McGregor), Pernell Roberts (B.J. Anderson), Robert Hogan (Coopersmith), Phillip Sterling (Thomas Nardoni), Simon Oakland (Vern St. Cloud), Paul Fix (Bill Tooley), Lou Krugman (Sam Detonis).

Rockford is joined by a novice detective, Richie Brockelman, as they investigate the suspicious traffic death of a fellow private eye. While comparing notes at the late Joe Tooley's funeral, Rockford and Brockelman agree that he would never be on the freeway, the scene of his death. So, backtracking on Tooley's last investigation, a case involving a city councilman's crooked dealings, they find an elaborate computer system at a house on Willis Avenue. This leads to conglomerate executive Garth McGregor, who through his sophisticated detecting devices, is a step ahead of them and now has plans for their demise.

(Note: Richie Brockelman, played by Dennis Dugan, reprises a role here that he played in a 1976 made-for-TV movie, *The Missing Twenty - Four Hours*, a film written and produced by Stephen J. Cannell and *Hill Street Blues* creator Steven Bochco. The episode also served as a jumping-off point for a short-lived series, *Richie Brockelman, Private Eye*, which occupied Rockford's Friday time slot for the next five weeks.)

James Garner in SUPPORT YOUR LOCAL SHERIFF, along with Joan Hackett, Walter Brennan, Harry Morgan and Jack Elam.

GARNER'S OTHER ROLES

James Garner and Mariette Hartley.

CHAPTER SIXTEEN:

THE EPISODES: FIFTH SEASON

Heartaches of A Fool

First telecast: Sept. 22, 1978

Director: William Wiard. Writer: Stephen J. Cannell.

Regular cast: Garner, Beery.

Guest cast: Taylor Lacher (Charlie Strayhorn), James Shigata (Clement Chen), Lynn Marta (Carrie Strayhorn), Mark Roberts (Hillman), Norman Alden (Roland Eddy), Herb Armstrong (Norman), Don "Red" Barry (Shorty McCall), George Kee Cheung (Harry Lee), Raymond O'Keefe (Jake Sand), Joe E. Tata (Norman Abbott Kline).

A famous singing cowboy's crooked managers involve him in an underworld war that threatens Rockford's father. Recording star Charlie Strayhorn has diversified interests including an Arkansas- based sausage company. Rocky becomes an innocent pawn in the war between members of a Chinese mob and Strayhorn's scheming business managers when mobsters cause his truck, loaded with sausage, to overturn and roll. Enter Rockford, who follows the trail back to an unsuspecting Strayhorn.

(Note: This episode's title song. *Heartaches of A Fool*, was written and performed by Willie Nelson.)

Rosendohl and Gilda Stern Are Dead

First telecast: Sept. 28. 1978

Director: William Wiard. Writer: Juanita Bartlett.

Regular cast: Garner, Beery, Santos.

Guest cast: Rita Moreno (Rita Capkovic), Abe Vigoda (Phil "the Dancer" Gabriel), Robin Gammell (Donald Pilmer), Robert Loggia (Russell Nevitt), William Joyce (Dr. Neil Rosendohl), John Karlen (Leo), Ron Gilbert (Freddie), Sharon Acker (Edie Nevitt).

Rita, a prostitute friend of Rockford, asks his help when she is threatened after witnessing an underworld murder. It seems her surgeon customer, Dr. Neil Rosendohl, was killed on orders from Phil the Dancer because the doctor botched his hip operation. Rita is arrested and charged with the slaying and it's up to Rockford to clear her and protect her from Phil, who wants all witnesses eliminated.

(Note: Rita Moreno, in her second appearance as Rita Capkovic, was nominated for a best actress honors but was beaten out by Mariette Hartley, James Garner's co-star in a series of Polaroid commercials. Hartley would appear in a Rockford episode and receive the best actress nomination the following season.)

The Jersey Bounce

First telecast: Oct. 6, 1978

Director: William Wiard. Writers: Juanita Bartlett, Stephen J. Cannell and David Chase.

Regular cast: Garner, Beery.

Guest cast: Bo Hopkins (John Cooper), Greg Antonacci (Eugene Conigliaro), Doney Oatman (David Nodzak), Luke Andreas (Artie Nodzak), Walter Olkweicz (Mac Amodeus).

Rockford is accused of beating a man to death at a party hosted by Eugene Conigliaro and Mickey Long, recent arrivals from New Jersey who have been harassing Rockford's father and his neighbors. It's a trumped-up charge, of course, but when Rockford hires high-priced attorney Wade Ward, he finds Ward incompetent. Ward's assistant, John Cooper, a disbarred attorney who can only do research now, is the one with the brains. Rockford and Cooper work as a team and even get help from an underworld source as they set out to clear Rockford's name.

(Note: Bo Hopkins, as John Cooper, makes his first appearance on *The Rockford Files*. He replaced Gretchen Corbett, who left the series after her four-year commitment was up. Hopkins' presence reunited him with Noah Beery. The two were regulars on *Doc Elliot* in 1974.)

White on White and Nearly Perfect

First telecast: Oct. 20, 1978

Director: Stephen J. Cannell. Writer: Stephen J. Cannell.

Regular cast: Garner, Beery, Santos.

Guest cast: Tom Selleck (Lance White), Carolyn Calcote (Angela), James Luisi (Lieutenant Chapman), Luis Delgado (Officer Billings), Frank Christi (Vincent), Peter Brocco (Meyer Ziegler), Eddie Fontaine (Augusto DePalma), Julienne Wells (Bella LaBelle), Karen Austin (Veronica Teasdale).

Rockford's search for an industrialist's missing daughter is complicated by the fact that a second private investigator is working the same case. Rockford's rival is Lance White, an affluent "Mr. Perfect" P.I. who behaves as if he were a hero in a crime novel and whose methods endanger both detective's lives. What initially appears to be a simple case of a girl running away with her lover turns into an international caper, in which the rich man's daughter is used as a bargaining pawn for an underworld financier's passage to Israel.

(Note: This episode marks the first appearance by Tom Selleck in the recurring role of Lance White. Selleck would later play Thomas Magnum in *Magnum P. I.*, a detective series that shared Rockford's tongue-in-cheek sense of humor. One episode—titled *Tigers Fan*—even had characters discussing a Rockford episode. Rockford regular Joe Santos would have a recurring role in that series, appearing in four episodes as

Lieutenant Nolan Page in 1987-88, and Rockford producer Charles Floyd Johnson would serve as its supervising producer in 1982-86 and co-executive producer in 1986-88.)

Kill the Messenger

First telecast: Oct. 27, 1978.

Director: Ivan Dixon. Writer: Juanita Bartlett.

Regular cast: Garner, Beery, Santos.

Guest cast: James Luisi (Lieutenant Chapman), Pat Finley (Peggy Becker), Byron Morrow (Chief Towne), W. K. Stratton (Lieutenant Frank Dusenberg), Ed Harris (Rudy Kempner), Luis Delgado (Officer Billings).

Rockford jeopardizes his friendship with Becker when he takes it upon himself to help investigate the slaying of Deputy Chief Towne's philandering wife. Though Towne assures Becker he wants no special treatment, it becomes increasingly sensitive when the unsavory character of the chief's wife is revealed—a development that makes Towne himself a leading suspect. Becker's burden is further complicated because he's busy studying for his lieutenant's exam and he's getting no help from his rookie partner, Dusenberg, preoccupied with his pregnant wife. But, Rockford's unsolicited help proves to be of great assistance when he stumbles onto a telltale clue.

(Note: Joe Santos singled this episode out as being his favorite Rockford. Luis Delgado, James Garner's longtime stand-in and friend, finally had a recurring role, as Officer Billings. Until this year he played a variety of small roles.)

The Empty Frame

First telecast: Oct. 3, 1978.

Director: Corey Allen. Writer: Steven J. Cannell.

Regular cast: Garner, Santos, Margolin.

Guest cast: Richard Romanus (Sean Innes), Robert Alda (Cy Marguilies), James Luisi (Lieutenant Chapman), Janis Paige (Miriam), Gilbert Green (Talib), Maria Grimm (Princess Khedra Aziz).

Rockford is hired to find a married Arabian princess and ultimately learns her family intends to kill her. Though Princess Khedra Aziz's husband is the philanderer, the princess is condemned to death by her family when she runs off with pseudo-writer Sean Innes. Rockford first finds Innes, a gigolo now living off wealthy Miriam, and forces him to find Khedra. Khedra was merely a pawn, but the princess' family still wants her to pay the supreme penalty for having shamed them. Rockford in turn finds himself protecting her.

A Good Clean Bust with Sequel Rights

First telecast: Nov. 17, 1978.

Director: William Wiard. Writer: Rudolph Borchert.

Regular cast: Garner, Beery, Santos.

Guest cast: Hank Brandt (Captain Lindner), Hector Elizondo (Frank Falcone), James Murtaugh (Bob Parsons), James B. Sikking (Jeff Seals), Jenny Sherman (Linda), Nicolas Coster (Augie Augustine), Louise Moritz (Debbi), Jerry Douglas (Wexler), Joana Lipari (Mrs. Stern).

Rockford is hired as bodyguard for former New York City cop Frank Falcone, now a legendary figure with a TV show and toys patterned after him. The job becomes hazardous when past enemies try to kill Falcone.

The toy manufacturers want Rockford to keep Falcone out of trouble until they can get their new line on the market, but Falcone's former police partner, Wexler, jealous of Falcone's public image, involves him in a fracas. Rockford's situation is complicated when underworld hit men from Illinois include Falcone in a contract. Rockford, caught in the middle, is fired from protecting his client but must continue to defend him to save his own life—since the mobsters think he is Falcon's friend.

Black Mirror

First telecast: Nov. 24, 1978 (120-minute episode).

Director: Arnold Laven. Writer: David Chase.

Regular cast: Garner, Beery, Santos, Margolin.

Guest cast: Kathryn Harrold (Dr. Megan K. Dougherty), John Pleshett (Danny Green/Jackie Tetuska), Leo V. Gordon (Charles Martell), Brian Cutler (Don Savio), Julia Ann Benjamin (Bonny), Jack Garner (Janitor), Alan Manson (Dr. Carl Rainier), Carl Franklin (Roger Orloff), Wallace Earl (Myra), Denny Miller (Norman).

Dr. Megan Dougherty, a beautiful blind psychologist, hires Rockford after being accosted in an elevator and later is troubled by phone calls. Rockford suspects one of Megan's unstable patients is responsible, but Megan refuses to divulge any professional secrets. Rockford, who is falling for Megan, calls on a handwriting expert who at least gives him a clue to one of her patients, Danny Green, whom Megan refuses to believe is violent. Rockford, therefore, finds himself in a dilemma. If he uncovers Danny as the assailant, he will reveal Megan's mistake in originally diagnosing her client. Ultimately, however, Rockford discovers that Green is in fact a professional killer, that he has been leading a double life in order to have a ready-made insanity defense should the police ever close in. Rockford must move fast now—because Green intends to set his "alibi" plan in motion by murdering Megan.

(Note: Kathryn Harrold makes her first of two appearances as Megan, who, if only briefly, becomes the most important woman in Rockford's life.)

A Fast Count

First telecast: Dec. 1, 1978.

Director: Reza S. Badiyi. Writer: Gordon Dawson.

Regular cast: Garner, Beery.

Guest cast: Ken McMillan (Morry Hawthorne), Mary Frann (Ruth), Rocky Echevarria (Jesus), Lawrence Casey (Don White), Len Wayland (Nelson), Bert Kramer (Skip LaForce), Don Starr (Kaplan).

When a fighter's manager is accused of bribery and homicide, Rockford, who owns a percentage of the boxer, investigates. Morry Hawthorne's troubles begin when authorities accuse him of leaving $5,000 in cash in their office to "resolve" fighter Jesus' immigration problems involving his grandmother-in-law. Morry's headaches get bigger shortly thereafter when he's slapped with a murder charge. Rockford's probe leads him to a woman who does TV commercials for a used-car dealership and somehow involves her attempts to buy Jesus' contract.

Local Man Eaten by Newspaper

First telecast: Dec. 8, 1978.

Director: Meta Rosenberg. Writer: Juanita Bartlett.

Regular cast: Garner, Beery, Santos.

Guest cast: Bo Hopkins (John Cooper), Scott Brady (Harrold Witbeck), Gianni Russo (Johnny Bongard), Pat Renelia (Vincent), Joseph Hindy (Leo), Luis Delgado (Officer Billings), Dallas Mitchell (Dr. Hagan), Harlee McBride (Monica).

Rockford becomes the target of a scandalous newspaper and underworld assassins when he investigates the shooting of a show business doctor. Dr. Hagan, who treats Hollywood's top stars, hires Rockford to find out who burglarized his office. The trail leads to the gossip-hungry *National Insider*, headed by editor Harold Witbeck. Real danger sets in, though, when Hagan is wounded in a second burglary of his office, an incident to which Rockford is a witness. Rockford now finds he is being slandered by the *Insider* and stalked by the mobster Augie Arno (under orders of mob boss Johnny Bongard.)

With the French Heel Back Can the Nehru Jacket Be Far Behind?"

First telecast: Jan. 5, 1979.

Director: Ivan Dixon. Writer: Rudolph Borchert.

Regular cast: Garner, Beery, Santos.

Guest cast: Rene Auberjonois (Masters), Erin Gray (Alta), Marissa Pavan (Sophia), Howard Witt (Bencroft), Chris Palmer (Carol), W. K. Stratton (Lieutenant Dusenberg), Albert Carrier (Monty).

Rockford enters the world of fashion when he suspects foul play after a model's death is written off by police as a suicide. Though it appears that the model, Carol, leaped from her hotel room window, Rockford knows better, based on an earlier call from her. His probe leads to a kinky new-wave designer, Masters, who was going to use Carol in his fashion show. Masters hires Rockford to investigate Carol's death and the possible theft of an original dress design. Getting help from Alta, a beautiful model-turned-lighting director, Rockford stumbles through the strange world of fashion as he tracks the culprit.

The Battle-Ax and the Exploding Cigar

First telecast: Jan. 12, 1979.

Director: Ivan Dixon. Writer: Rogers Turrentine (from Mann

Rubin and Michael Wagner's story).

Regular cast: Garner, Beery.

Guest cast: Marge Redmond (Eleanor), Glenn Corbett (Spelling), Lane Smith (Donnegan), Dawson Mays (Tony Musia), Antoine Becker (Stacy), Sully Boyar (Petrankus), Lindsay V. Jones (Susan), Roscoe Born (Tallafero), Charles Weldon (Watkins), Mitzi Hoag (Margaret), Mary-Nancy Burnett (Jill), Kirk Mae (Pearce).

Rockford loses his shirt gambling in Las Vegas. Broke and stranded, he gets a lift back to Los Angeles from a friendly stranger on the condition that he help out by doing part of the driving. Turns out, however, that the car is stolen and has a truckload of weapons. The car is stopped by a couple of inquisitive cops and Rockford, naturally, is arrested on charges of gun-running and grand theft auto. When he's freed on bail, he sets out to discover why he's been framed and finds it's all part of a big puzzle involving a renegade band of intelligence operatives selling defective weapons to Third World revolutionaries.

Guilt

First telecast: Jan. 19, 1979.

Director: William Wiard. Writer: Juanita Bartlett.

Regular cast: Garner, Beery, Santos.

Guest cast: Pat Crowley (Valerie), Robert Quarry (Joe Zakarian), Rita Gam (Cynthia), Elizabeth Brooks (Jean Ludwig), Ted Shackleford (Eric Genther), Eldon Quick (Singleton), James Lough (Brian Tegg), Luis Delgado (Officer Billings), Timothy Wayne (Allen Hough), Ben Young (Goldstone).

Rockford's former girlfriend, Valerie, is being terrorized, apparently without motive. Rockford agrees to investigate a shooting attempt on Valerie, which occurred when she was walking her dog on the beach. He finds himself forced into a painful side trip down memory lane. But the reopening of emotional wounds—something Valerie is particular adept at doing—is nothing compared to the danger he faces when caught in a deadly game of blackmail and inter-family treachery.

The Deuce

First telecast: Jan. 26, 1979.

Director: Benard McEveety. Writer: Gordon Dawson.

Regular cast: Garner, Beery.

Guest cast: Mills Watson (George Bassett), Sharon Spelman (Karen Hathaway), Patricia Hindy (Fran Bassett), Margaret Blye (Bonnie), Richard Kelton (Norman Wheeler), Edward Walsh (Van Sickle), Joe Maross (Corbett).

Jury duty leads to danger when Rockford stubbornly refuses to believe an alcoholic is guilty of vehicular manslaughter. Rockford soon finds himself trying to unravel a puzzle involving the bogus sister of the dead girl, a legal secretary, and a prominent attorney who hires an unscrupulous private eye to silence anyone who threatens to uncover the lawyer's criminal activities.

(Note: This episode appeared on a Thursday this day only.)

The Man Who Saw Alligators

First telecast: Feb. 10, 1979 (90 - minute episode).

Director: Corey Allen. Writer: David Chase.

Regular cast: Garner, Beery, Santos, Margolin.

Guest cast: George Loros (Anthony Boy), Luke Andreas (Sly), Sharon Acker (Adriana Danielli), Joey Aresco (Richie Gagglio), Joseph Sirola (Joe Minett), Penny Santon (Ma Gagglio), Julie Parrish (Jeannie), Lavina Dawson (Conchatta), Joseph Perry (Murt), Marc Bentley (Ethan), Joseph Perry (Murt Guellow).

Anthony Boy, a Brooklyn gangster caught "doing a job" in California, has a score to settle with Rockford. Now released from prison, Anthony craves revenge, despite encouragement from his mother, Ma Gagglio, to come back home, where mob boss Joe Minett has a place for him. Anthony stubbornly remains in California, looking for Rockford. That's when Angel comes into the picture, blabbing the location of Rockford's hideout, Lake Arrowhead. Now it's a matter of who will strike first: Anthony against Rockford or the mob hit men who have been dispatched to kill Anthony.

(Note: With this episode the series was moved to a Saturday time slot, where it remained until Friday, March 13, 1979, when *A Different Drummer*, the last new episode of the season, was telecast. George Loros, as Anthony Boy, and Luke Andreas, as Sly, reprise roles they first played in *To Protect and Serve*.

The Return of the Black Shadow

First telecast: Feb. 17, 1979.

Director: William Wiard. Writer: Stephen J. Cannell

Regular cast: Garner, Beery, Santos.

Guest cast: Bo Hopkins (John Cooper), Paul Koslo (Whispering Willie), Dennis Burkley (Thomas "Animal" Nicholas), Laurie Jefferson (Gail Cooper), Andy Jerrell (Phil Dankus), Paul Mace (Chester "Festus" Blake), Jerry Ayes (Robert Greis).

What starts out as a simple date between Rockford and Gail Cooper, a college physics researcher who is the sister of John Cooper, takes a tragic turn when the Rattlers, a motorcycle gang lead by Whispering Willie, strike. The Rattlers attack at a gas station, roughing up Rockford and kidnapping Gail. Rockford manages to get a license plate number and, with this clue, begins his investigation. Cooper—a former member of the rampaging Black Shadow gang—sets out to infiltrate the Rattlers, with designs on evening the score.

A Material Difference

First telecast: Feb. 24, 1979.

Director: William Wiard. Writer: Rogers Turentine.

Regular cast: Garner, Beery, Santos, Margolin.

Guest cast: Michael, McGuire (Bernard), David Tress (Bert), James Luisi (Lieutenant Chapman), Michael Aldredge (Dobson), Joshua Bryant (Holt), John Davey (Cowboy), Rod Browning (Leonard), Donald Bishop (Randolph).

Rockford finds himself mixed up in another of Angel's half-baked scams. Angel has been posing as a hit man. His plan is to collect half the fee up front for murders he has no intention of committing, then disappear before the customer realizes he's been taken. This plan hits a snag with the first customer, a Russian undercover agent who wants a defector believed to be holding a secret formula assassinated. When Rockford learns of Angel's scheme, he tries to untangle it, but agents from Russia, as well as U.S. Navy Intelligence, are hot on their trail, thinking Angel and Rockford have run off with the all-important formula.

Never Send A Boy King To Do A Man's Job

First telecast: March 3, 1979 (120 - minute episode).

Director: William Wiard. Writer: Juanita Bartlett.

Regular cast: Garner, Beery, Margolin.

Guest cast: Dennis Dugan (Richie Brockelman), Robert Webber (Harold Jack Coombs), Trisha Noble (Odette), Harold Gould (Mr. Brockelman), Kim Hunter (Mrs. Brockelman), David Hooks (Doyle), Gary Crosby (Larry Litrell), Todd Martin (Nesbitt/Wendkos), Stanley Brook (Cowboy Martell), Pepper Martin (Harry Steel), Jack Collins (Dr. Wetherford), Stephanie Hankinson (Toulie), Michele Hart (Maggie), Robert Ward (B. J.).

When Richie Brockelman learns his parents have been cheated by unscrupulous businessman Harold Jack Coombs, pressuring the elder Brockelman into selling his business for a fraction of its value, Richie calls on Rockford, his former mentor, for help. Initially reluctant to get involved, Rockford finally gives in and the two concoct a gigantic con requiring Rockford to assume one of his favorite false identities, that of Jimmy Joe Meeker, Oklahoma oilman. Calling on a former Coombs victim, race driver Larry Litrell, "Jimmy Joe" and Richie put their plan in motion. They first take Coombs' race car away in a "match" race, then maneuver him through a slippery maze involving an Egyptian art show as elaborate as the King Tut exhibition.

(Note: This episode is also known as **The Return of Richie Brockelman**.)

A Different Drummer

First telecast: March 13, 1979

Director: Reza S. Badiyi. Writer: Rudolph Borchert.

Regular cast: Garner, Beery, Santos.

Guest cast: John Considine (Dr. Lee Yost), Jesse Welles (Sorel), Reni Santoni (Perry), Lesley Qoosa (Lucy Grange), Harlan Warde (Evan Grange), Walter Brooke (Dr. Bosca), Carmen Argenziano (Dunes), Patrick Culliton (Patrolman), Anne Bellamy (Nurse), Will Gill Jr. (Orderly).

While hospitalized after being involved in an auto accident, Rockford stumbles onto what appears to be an illegal organ-transplant ring. Groggy from sedatives, Rockford accidentally wanders into a room where Dr. Yost is extracting an organ from a donor. When Rockford sees the cadaver move his arm during the operation, he becomes convinced foul play is afoot. He questions hospital doctors, who dismiss the incident flippantly. No one seems to take his charges seriously. On his release, Rockford pursues the investigation and discovers Yost is masterminding the scheme for his highly profitable organ-transplant foundation and that murder is just one of the means he'll use to find donors.

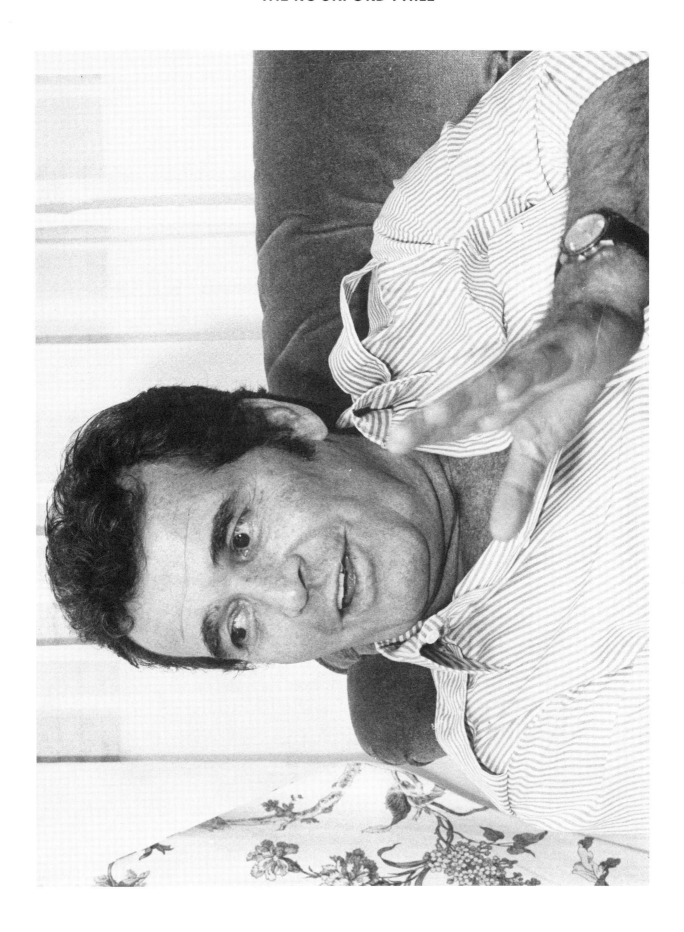

Dennis Dugan and James Garner.

CHAPTER SEVENTEEN:

THE EPISODES: SIXTH SEASON

Paradise Cove

First telecast: Sept. 28, 1979

Director: Stephen J. Cannell. Writer: Stephen J. Cannell

Regular cast: Garner, Beery, Santos, Margolin

Guest cast: Mariette Hartley (Althea Morgan), Leif Erickson (C. C. Calloway), Raymond O'Keefe (Jake Sand), Byron Morrow (Don McLinton), Frederick Herrick (Cliff Calloway), Christine Avila (Nurse), John Davey (Rudy), Peter Brocco (Roscoe), Luis Delgado (Officer Billings).

Nothing but trouble for Rockford. Seems his car struck his Paradise Cove Trailer Colony neighbor, retired sheriff C.C. Calloway, a man who had an unfriendly relationship with Rockford in the first place. C. C. sues Rockford for a whopping $35,000 and wins. Only Rockford's stone broke. Enter Althea Morgan, a tough court-appointed receiver who sets up shop in Rockford's mobile home to inventory his meager assets and help find a way to pay. C. C., meanwhile, is organizing a movement to have Rockford ousted from Paradise Cove. Althea steps in with the suggestion that Rockford become Paradise Cove's new night watchman. The job doesn't pay much, but it does get Rockford involved with suspicious trespassers, a 50-year-old whiskey-smuggling case and a search for lost gold. When it appears that C. C. was involved in some of the illegal shenanigans, Althea joins Rockford in an attempt to bring the old codger to justice.

(Note: Mariette Hartley co-starred with James Garner for years in a series of popular Polaroid commercials before this episode. Said Hartley: "I auditioned three or four times before on Rockford and they wouldn't touch me before those commercials came along." Hartley was nominated for an "Outstanding Lead Actress" Emmy for her appearance.)

Lions, Tigers, Monkeys and Dogs

First telecast: Oct. 12 1979 (120-minute episode).

Director: William Wiard. Writer: Juanita Bartlett.

Regular cast: Garner, Beery, Santos.

Guest cast: Lauren Bacall (Kendall Warren), Dana Wynter (Princess Irene Rachevsky), Corinne Michaels (Linda Hassler), Ed Nelson (Blake Sternlight), Michael Lombard (August "Gus" Fairfield), Carmine Caridi (Tommy Minette), James Luisi (Lieutenant Chapman), Michael Des Barres (Gordon Flack), Jack Garner (Captain McEnroe), Luis Delgado (Officer Billings), Melody Thomas (Sherry), Roger Til (Henri Tayir), Christopher Thomas (Freddie Danzig), T. Miratti (Paul Juliano Jr.) Leo V. Gordon (Charles Martell).

Princess Rachevsky is worried about Kendall Warren, believing her close friend's life is in danger. The princess hires Rockford to serve as her bodyguard. As soon Rockford takes the case, an attempt is made. Rockford makes a big social splash at a masquerade party by saving Kendall from a knife-wielding assailant costumed as a friar. (Rockford, incidentally, is dressed as an old-world scholar, complete with flowing robe and mortarboard.) Kendall writes the attack off as an attempted robbery, but Rockford takes the matter far more seriously. As their mystery deepens, so does the relationship between Rockford and Kendall.

(Note: James Garner and Lauren Bacall also co-starred in *H.E.A.L.T.H.*, a 1979 motion picture directed by Robert Altman. Two years later, Bacall and Garner would co-star in *The Fan*, a 1981 slasher film. Bacall was nominated for an "Outstanding Lead Actress" Emmy for her appearance in this episode.)

Only Rock 'n Roll Will Never Die

First telecast: Oct. 12 and Oct. 19, 1979 (two-part episode)

Director: William Wiard. Writer: David Chase.

Regular cast: Garner, Beery, Santos.

Guest cast: Kristoffer Tabori (Tim Richie), George Loros (Eddie), Marcia Strassman (Whitney Cox), Leigh Christian (Diane Bjornstrom), Jean Paul Vignon (Alain Floria), Alain Chappuis (Honore Florio), Lenny Baker (Ronny), Jack Garner (Captain McEnroe), Stanley Brock (Bernie Salkow), Fred Carney (Mitchell Robinson), Laurie Lea Schaefer (Lindy), Jesse Dizon (Jerry Ito), Marion Yue (Chiyoko Takai), Luis Delgado (Officer Billings).

Rock star Tim Richie's life is in shambles. His former live-in girlfriend is suing him for half his $30 million fortune, mobsters are bootlegging his latest album and a female reporter is dogging his steps. Richie's greatest concern, however, is that his best friend, a record producer, is missing. Rockford gets the call from Richie through Eddie, a former prison pal who now is Richie's security chief. Rockford has reason to believe the man's disappearance may be tied to the bootlegging operation and Rockford thoroughly investigates that angle. Someone even takes a few potshots at Rockford and Eddie to scare them off the case. When the missing man turns up murdered and Diane, Richie's ex, unwittingly reveals her knowledge of the incident, it appears the crime may turn out to have an unlikely link to the palimony case.

Love is the Word

First telecast: Nov. 9, 1979.

Director: John Patterson. Writer: David Chase.

Regular cast: Garner, Beery.

Guest cast: Kathryn Harrold (Megan Dougherty), Anthony Herrera (Jeffrey Smith), David-James Carroll (Randy Smith), Richard Cox (Lenny Spector), Van Williams (Lieutenant Duane Kefir), David Cadiente (Keith Keoloha), Betty Kennedy (Patty), Barbara Mandrell (Rayette).

Rockford returns from an out-of-town case and renews his romance with his blind girlfriend, Megan. He senses she has grown distant. It turns out she's been seeing another man, architect Jeffrey Smith. In fact, they're to be married soon, but Smith becomes the prime suspect in a murder and disappears. Megan asks Rockford to find him and prove his innocence. Rockford accepts the assignment, but not with purest of motives. He really would rather prove Smith's guilt, thereby eliminating a rival. During the investigation, in fact, the love affair between Rockford and Megan resumes. Before long, Rockford finds that Smith's brother, Randy, a doped-up deadbeat, is the source of the troubles. Rockford ultimately finds that love affairs can take peculiar turns as he loses Megan forever.

Nice Guys finish Dead

First telecast: Nov. 16, 1979

Director: John Patterson. Writer: Stephen J. Cannell.

Regular cast: Garner.

Guest cast: Tom Selleck (Lance White), James Whitmore Jr. (Fred Beamer), Simon Oakland (Vern St. Cloud), Larry Manetti (Larry St. Cloud), Erica Hagen (Brandy Alexander), James Luisi (Lieutenant Chapman), Joe Bernard (Carmine DeAngelo), Fritzi Burr (Mrs. DeAngelo), John Roselius (Mike Mikelson), Fred Lerner (Carl Richman), Al Berry (Ed Fuller), Larry Dunn (Norm Cross).

Attending the annual Private Detectives Association awards dinner, Rockford encounter a number of his old friends and rivals. There's Lance White, the dashing Mr. Perfect. There's Fred Beamer, the nerdy ex-auto mechanic who finally got his detective's license. There's even scuzzball Vern St. Cloud and his son, Larry. Rockford and Lance are up for the prestigious Goodhue Trophy, awarded annually to the "private investigator of the year." When Beamer leaves Rockford and Lance's table to go the men's room, he discovers the body of the guest speaker—murdered. Typically, Beamer panics and flees the scene, thereby becoming the leading suspect. Rockford and Lance, then, must work together—despite slight jealousy over the award—to clear Beamer.

(Note: Rockford won the Goodhue Trophy, in of the rare episodes in which he got the credit he rightly deserved. Somewhat typically, though, he lost the statuette later that night in an empty field. Also true to character, Lance White lived a storybook ending to his storybook existence on *The Rockford Files*. He married a beautiful heiress. Guests Tom Selleck and Larry Manetti later would work together for eight years in starring and supporting roles on *Magnum, P.I.*

The Hawaiian Headaches

First telecast: Nov. 23, 1979.

Director: William Wiard. Writer: Stephen J. Cannell.

Regular cast: Garner, Beery, Santos, Margolin.

Guest cast: Ken Swofford ("Howling Mad" Smith), James Murtaugh (Gordon Lyle), W. K. Stratton (Dwight Whipple), Christopher Cary (Dutch Ingram), Daniel Kamekona (Sergeant Okamoto), Jack Garner (Captain McEnroe), Luis Delgado (Officer Billings), Esmond Chung (Shawn Kimotto), Jake Hoopai (Benny Kimotto), Julie Blissett (Mrs. Ingram), Jimmy Borges (Marshal Mingus).

The Rockfords win a Hawaiian vacation, but when they arrive, Jim is shanghaied into a dangerous intelligence caper. Rockford's old Korean War commander, "Howling Mad" Smith, and his government agents grab Rockford at the airport, leaving Rocky standing there, alone and confused. Later, when Rocky catches his son eavesdropping with a glass on the hotel room wall, he shows his disgust, unaware that Rockford is in fact on a sensitive assignment. Rockford soon finds himself hip deep in trouble when the agent assigned to work with him is slain, leaving him at the mercy of double-dealing spy Dutch Ingram.

The No-Fault Affair

First telecast: Nov. 30, 1979.

Director: Corey Allen. Writer: Juanita Bartlett.

Regular cast: Garner, Santos, Margolin.

Guest cast:Rita Moreno (Rita Capkovic), Jerry Douglas (Al Halusca), Corrine Michaels (Linda Hassler), Pat Finley (Peggy Becker), William Beckley (Mr. Norman), Gloria Calomee (Hildy).

Prostitute Rita Capkovic decides the time is right to leave the streets and launch a career as a hairdresser. Her sadistic pimp has other ideas, subjecting her to a savage beating. Rockford asks Rita to stay at his trailer where he can protect her, but Rita misinterprets the invitation and—to Rocky's mortification—falls in love. Though Rockford thinks he can handle the situation, Rocky hovers over the two like a sorority-house mother. Rockford, meanwhile, sets out to make sure the pimp won't cause further troubles for Rita.

The Big Cheese

First telecast: Dec. 7, 1978

Director: Joseph Pevney. Writer: Shei Williams

Regular cast: Garner, Berry, Santos.

Guest cast: Constance Towers (Sally Packard), James Luisi (Lieutenant Chapman), Alan Manson (Chuck Ryan), George Pentecost (George Neff), Brian J. Pevney (Allan Calder), Hank Bradt (Sergeant Floyd), Ben Andrews (Stamps), Mark Lonow (Coco), Peter Hobbs (Walter Winterwood).

An alcoholic reporter working on a mob-union expose is murdered shortly after mailing the evidence to his friend Rockford, but the package is lost in the mail. While mob figures camp on Rockford's doorstep awaiting the mailman—at one point even assaulting him—Rockford joins forces with reporter Sally Packard as they attempt to trace the package before the mobsters can get their mitts on it. An outrageous twist—the package that was mailed to Rockford turned out not to be the evidence at all. It was just a giant wheel of cheese.

(Note: In this, his last episode, Lieutenant Chapman, Rockford's favorite foil, is dealt perhaps his most humiliating blow. Seems Chapman's about to be audited by the IRS and throughout the episode he's busily doctoring his tax records, on which he cheated big time. At the end of the episode, when he pops off to Rockford and Sally Packard that the IRS guys haven't got the smarts to catch him, Sally reveals a secret that even Rockford didn't know until well into the case: Sally is really an IRS investigator—and Chapman can count on extra scrutiny come audit time.)

Just A Coupla Guys

First telecast: Dec. 14, 1978

Director: Ivan Dixon. Writer: David Chase.

Regular cast: Garner.

\Guest cast: Greg Antonacci (Gene Coniglio), Gene Davis (Mickey Long), Gilbert Green (Joe Lombard), Lisa Donaldson (Renee Lombard), Gilbert Green (Beppy Conigliaro), Anthony Ponzini (Tony Martine), Doug Tobey (Anthony Martine), Robin Riker (Kathlene O'Meara), Jennifer Rhodes (Jean Martine), Arch Johnson (Cardinal Finnerty.)

Rockford is not only out of his territory, but out of luck when he flies to Newark, N.J., and discovers his assignment there involves the underworld and two young minor mob hustlers trying to make a reputation for themselves. On arriving, Rockford's watch and rental car are stolen and he is delayed at police headquarters. When he finally meets his employer, Renee Lombard, he learns she wants him to protect her father, a mob leader who was recently "born again." Problems arise when the young toughs, Gene and Mickey, inadvertently upset the underworld balance of power and Renee winds up kidnapped by an opposing gang. Rockford, then, is compelled to rescue her.

Deadlock in Parma

First telecast: Jan. 10, 1980

Director: Winrich Kolbe. Writer: Donald L. Gold, Lester

William Berke and Rudolph Borchert.

Regular cast: Garner.

Guest cast: Sandra Kerns (Carrie Osgood), Joseph Siola (Henry Gersh), Ben Piazza (Stan Belding), Michael Cavanaugh (John Trayner), Henry Beckman (Sheriff Neal), Jerry Hardin (Mayor Sindell).

While on a fishing trip, Rockford is duped into serving as proxy for his friend, a small-town councilman, in an upcoming referendum. He suddenly finds himself caught between two factions vying for control of the village of Parma for gambling and land development. Everyone from town officials to crooks to cops tries to turn the screws on Rockford, who must cast the deciding vote. Every time he tries to slip out of town, he gets rustled up and brought back. After a murder is committed as part of a plot by one of the factions to control his vote, Rockford is aided in his efforts to solve the crime by his new-found friend, reporter Carrie Osgood.

(Note): This episode, the last new Rockford installment to air on network television, was shown on a Thursday.)

The Mayor's Committee from Deer Lick Falls

Not telecast by network.

Director: Ivan Dixon. Writer: William Stratton.

Regular cast: Garner, Beery, Santos, Margolin.

Guest cast: Edward Binns (Everett Benson), Priscilla Barnes (Lauren Ingeborg), Charles Aidman (Noah Deitweiler), Jerry Hardin (Knute Jacobs), James Luisi (Lieutenant Chapman).

A quartet of innocent-looking businessmen from Deer Lick Falls, Mich., approach Rockford, hoping to hire him to find a used fire truck. The committee, headed by Ev Benson, really wants to commission Rockford to murder Lauren Ingeborg, a young woman who revealed their tax -dodge game to the IRS. Lauren left Deer Lick Falls some months earlier to pursue an acting career under an assumed name. Rockford turns down the assignment, then sets out to find Lauren before the committee can find someone who will do the job.

(Note: This episode, originally scheduled to air Nov. 25, 1977, was preempted and never rescheduled for a network appearance. In most syndication runs, the episode usually appears between *Irving the Explainer* and *Hotel of Fear*.)

CHAPTER EIGHTEEN:

THE LOST ROCKFORDS

When *The Rockford Files* shut down production at the end of November 1979 because of James Garner's ailing health, the season's intended docket of episodes were far from complete. Only ten episodes had been filmed. There were more scripts, ready to go before the camera, that would never see the light of day.

They were the lost Rockfords, so to speak. Granted, they weren't lost in the same sense that episodes of *The Honeymooners*, *Bonanza* or *I Love Lucy* had been—locked away and forgotten for years in some film vault—but it's a shame we'll never be able to view and enjoy these cases.

After all, two such scripts—*Never Trust A Boxx Boy*, by Stephen Cannell, and *Some People Are Trouble*, by Shel Williams —are quite good. In fact, Cannell's story, featuring yet another of Angel Martin's bollixed scams, is an absolute gem. It very likely could have become the classic Rockford episode.

Here, then, is the first look at those "lost" Rockfords:

SOME PEOPLE ARE TROUBLE

An aging ex-con, Aubrey P. Spotwood, is released from San Quentin after having served a 23-year sentence for the murder of his wife. To this day, however, he contends his wife is still alive, that he had been framed, and he vows to find her. He turns to Rockford for help.

Spotwood: "I'd like you to find my wife. I didn't kill her. I want you to prove that so I can inherit her estate."

Rockford: "I'm sorry, Mr. Spotwood, but I really couldn't take on a case like yours right now."

Spotwood: "Why not?"

Rockford: "Because I'm not stupid, that's why. You can't even afford to pay me."

Spotwood: "I'll give you the pink slip on my car and we can make some sort of arrangement concerning a percentage of Leora's estate."

Rockford: "It's too flimsy, Mr. Spotwood. I don't work for percentages. I can't pay my bills with them."

But Rockford is given two reasons to take the case.

First Rocky practically begs his son to take it: "When Mrs. Spotwood disappeared, picking up the paper every morning (back then) was like reading a mystery story. Everybody was trying to figure out what he done with her and when Spotwood finally went to prison, it was real disappointing. I mean, it was kind of like they left the last chapter out of the book."

But money, not his father's curiosity, proves to be Rockford's real motivation: It seems Leora Spotwood's estate amounts to about $11 million.

Rockford: "Eleven million? I think you mentioned something about the pink slip of your car as collateral."

Rockford's investigation first brings him to a Mrs. Iris Curzon, executor of the Spotwood estate. But Rockford leaves with no more answers than when he first arrived—a fact he finds particularly aggravating when he goes home, only to find Rocky and a friend inside the trailer.

Rockford: "Did we have some kind of plans?"

Rocky: "No. Nothing like that. We was just waiting on a

progress report. I bet you didn't even know that old L. J. here

almost got himself chose as an alternate juror at Spotwood's

trial."

L. J.: "The D.A. was prejudiced against plumbers."

Rockford: "That's too bad, L. J., but I'm afraid there isn't going to be any progress report."

Rocky: "How come, Jimmy?"

Rockford: "Because I didn't make any progress."

Rockford's on the verge of throwing in the towel until a new development. It seems Spotwood has been hospitalized after an apparent hit-and-run attempt.

At the hospital, Rockford learns from Becker the incident is being investigated not as a premeditated murder attempt, but as a run-of-the-mill "hit-and-split." Becker adds a curious detail: "Your client was carrying a can of eight-millimeter porno film when he got bounced."

When Rockford sees Spotwood, the old man insists the incident was a deliberate attempt on his life. He says a black limousine came up over the curb after him.

Rockford: "If you'll excuse me for asking, who'd want to kill you?"

Spotwood: "My wife—or somebody who's trying to stop me from finding her."

It's a notion that keeps Rockford from giving up just yet.

The only fresh possibility, the porno film Spotwood claims was mailed to him to lure him into being a target, brings Rockford to the office of Homer Garrett, an ex-movie censor who now heads a group called Straight Citizens Against Trash.

Rockford, naturally, has assumed a bogus identity. He introduces himself as Bullock, an author "devoting an entire chapter" to Garrett and his organization. Garrett, naturally, is only too happy to oblige. It seems Garrett's background has made him an expert.

Garrett is able to identify the film, which features a big- breasted ballerina, as a 1955 cheapo called *Pink Tights*.

Garrett: "This film was made by Frank Pine, a very strange type who showed up on the local porno scene about 25 years ago."

Rockford: "What's so strange about him?"

Garrett: "Oh, there were all kinds of weird stories. Pine showed up out of nowhere and made this film. Then he just suddenly dropped out and so did every single person who had dealings with him."

Rockford: "You make him sound like some kind of mass murderer."

It's a notion that leads Rockford to Becker, asking for information on Pine. It seems Pine character was connected to six murders about 25 years earlier. The victims were young women, ages 18 to 25, all of them mixed up in the porno business. All of the bodies were found dressed in ballerina costumes.

Becker: "All of them had their skulls crushed. The killings were unofficially know in the department as the work of the Crusher."

Rockford's on to something now—and he really knows he's turned over the right rock when, that evening, he's awakened in bed by loud crashing noises. He scrambles outside to find two thugs brutalizing his car with tire irons. Then one of the thugs lets Rockford have it. "You wanna get out of the Spotwood case, brother. You just forget all about it—or the next time we bust you up instead of your ride."

Rockford's in a surly mood now—and he first takes his frustration out on Spotwood, who he believes withheld more than a few facts of the case. Seems Rockford studied up by reading old newspaper clippings and the circumstantial evidence against Spotwood—including a freshly dug grave in the Spotwood cellar—was very convincing indeed.

Rockford: "You've just run a couple of hummers by me. I'm going to give you one more chance to tell me the truth."

Spotwood: Leora and I had been married for nearly 10 years before I learned she had betrayed me practically from our wedding night with a staggering variety of partners. I decided to take her life. I prepared a list of what I would need to dispose of the body and personally prepared her final resting place."

Rockford: "And she found out about it?"

Spotwood: "Exactly. She disappeared before I could carry out my plans, but she left me with all that damning evidence for the district attorney to use."

Later that evening, after another somewhat unproductive day on the case, Rockford is home watching television, *The Dick Cavett Show*, and Cavett's guest is Sybil Trelawny, an aging romance novelist with big breasts. Rockford recognizes her as the ballerina in the porno film.

The following morning Rockford drives Rocky's truck to the mansion of Sybil Trelawny. He spots a dented black limo in the garage. But he's too late. The woman has been brutally murdered. It looks like the Crusher has come out of retirement.

Later that morning Rockford starts poking around the abandoned Spotwood mansion. During this visit, he again is attacked by the men who trashed his car, but this time Rockford manages to hold his own and his would-be assailants split. In the scuffle, though, one of the thugs loses an ankh (a cross with a loop at the top).

It's a symbol that we and Rockford had seen earlier—on the estate of Mrs. Iris Curzon. From Mrs. Curzon, Rockford learns that Mrs. Spotwood is indeed still alive. Pressured, she tells him where to find her, at a "spiritual center" in Venice. Calif. Once there he meets Sister Lilly, the long-missing Mrs. Spotwood. The two thugs are there, but Lilly sends them away.

Lilly: "I've been expecting you, Mr. Rockford. Dear Iris said you were an intelligent young man. My husband had the ability to spot talent in people. I'm afraid there was little else to recommend about him."

Rockford: "He doesn't speak too well of you either."

Lilly: "Of course, he doesn't. I discovered his secret."

Rockford: "What secret?"

Lilly: "The young women. There were six of them. He killed

them all, you know."

Rockford: "I don't think so. A man named Frank Pine killed

them."

Lilly: "My husband is Frank Pine."

That explains everything, including the recent murder of Sybil Trelawny, who had tried to strike first with her limo. And in the midst of their conversation, in steps Spotwood, a gun in hand. Seems he had followed Rockford.

Spotwood: "You're an imbecile, Rockford. They said in prison that you were a man who knew how to do this job and keep his mouth shut. They also said you could be easily duped with just about any halfway reasonable story."

It looks like curtains for Lilly and Rockford. But just as Old Man Spotwood's about to pull the trigger, he keels over from a coronary.

Rockford's being interviewed on television for solving the Leora Spotwood case. Rocky can be seen in the background, the button-popping proud papa. And though he won't be collecting a percentage on the $11 million Spotwood estate, at least Rockford isn't stiffed entirely. After all, he holds the title to Spotwood's car, a mint-condition 1955 Cadillac.

Which is when company comes, a man in a cowboy hat.

Cowboy: "I run the Classic Car Museum in Tustin. I spotted that old Cad. They said it belonged to you now."

Rockford: "You wouldn't be interested in buying it, would you?"

Cowboy: "Nope, I'm only interested in getting my hands on the $3,200 Old Man Spotwood owes me for storing his car for the last 23 years. I guess this (bill) belongs to you now."

Screwed again.

NEVER TRUST A BOXX BOY

Welcome to the palatial Beverly Hills estate of Marty Boxx, a Hollywood talent agent who's the biggest in the business—literally. He's fatter than Jabba the Hut and his list of clients is longer than his waistline. The only thing bigger still is the enormity of his ego.

Marty has been bedridden with a case of phlebitis but his bedroom is swarming with Hollywood types—a producer named Jerry Joseph, a writer named Jerry Martinson, a director named Marty Matz—and Marty's doctor, Jerry Keiser. It seems the dizzying array of Marty's and Jerry's are scripting a motion picture, one based on a true-life adventure Marty Boxx is still in the process of acting out.

Boxx: "Do you really think Marlon is right to play me? After all, we are talking about a classic. Orson, if he's shaven, could do it."

Because of Marty Boxx's inability to get around, he's had one of his junior agents, a recent hire named Marty Martain, sent over to serve as his gopher around the house.

In walks Angel Martin.

Angel (the kiss-up): "Maaaartttty. How good to finally meet you, I'm Marty Martain. You, sir, if I may, have been an absolute inspiration to talent agentry everywhere. Your heavy-handed, brutish, uncompromising, up-the-nose style of negotiating has made me, personally, stand in awe, Marty."

Boxx: "You will call me 'sir' or 'Mr. Boxx.'"

With Angel put in his place, Boxx and his entourage get back to business. Though it's not clear yet what their film is about, we learn that Boxx has a rendezvous scheduled that evening with "the Kirovs." Boxx vows to make the appoint-ment, despite his phlebitis, but there's a new complication. The chauffeur hasn't shown up.

Angel gets elected to do the driving. And off they go in the night—riding in Rockford's car.

En route to the rendezvous, Angel learns some more about the project at hand.

Angel: "Marty—Mr. Boxx—I'm having some trouble understanding what's going on. See, I mean, are you doing a movie about yourself or something?"

Boxx: "A movie about myself? Like some egotistical actor who wants to see himself on a screen? I don't do vain, silly things. It's just that every now and then a person finds himself in a drama that asks to be written. No, no. Demands to be written."

Angel: "So we're not making a movie?"

Boxx: "Of course, we're making a movie. And we're living the script, a script that will be written tomorrow. Maybe we should get a dramatic license. We might get Raquel to play you, have her wear something low-cut."

Angel (lapping it up): "I like De Niro better than Raquel. If you want my opinion, De Niro do me good. We just tell him not to scream too much."

While waiting outside a municipal music center, Marty Boxx now reveals to Angel that the rendezvous involves a political defection.

Angel: "The Kirovs? Who are the Kirovs?"

Boxx: "Who are the Kirovs? You're a Boxx Boy, working in the most prestigious talent agency on earth, and you ask a question like that?"

Angel: "Wait a minute. Sure, the Kirovs. Yeah, the Kirovs. At first I didn't hear you right. I've been having this inner ear problem."

Boxx: "You don't even know who they are."

Angel: "Tumblers, right? The Flying Kirovs? Acrobats. They work with a trampoline and hoops."

Boxx: "Russian ballet dancers."

Then they show up. Anton and Nina Kirov. Marty struggles to step out of the Firebird, calling to them. The Kirovs hustle over, but just then a host of armed men try to stop them. Anton and Nina get in the car just as shots are fired. Angel, chicken-hearted to the end, revs the motor and drives away—leaving Marty Boxx behind.

Another car gives chase. Angel heads straight to Rockford's place. Anton and Nina are asking Angel questions in Russian.

Angel: "Look, buddy. Stop gibbering at me, okay? You and the skirt just take off, okay? We're quits, punto e basta, hasta luego, adios."

Angel enters Rockford's trailer—no sign of Rockford—and makes a phone call, hoping to arrange someplace to hide out. As he looks out the window he sees the car that had been following him pull up. Angel turns out the lights. Bullets are flying, tearing holes in the paneling of the trailer.

Angel hustles back outside to the car and makes tracks, leaving the helpless Kirov couple in his dust. The gunmen take the couple captive.

Now we finally see Rockford. He's taking it easy at some remote fishing lodge in the country. There's a television on in the background, a reporter recounting the details of the Kirov kidnapping.

Reporter: "In a strange development in the case, authorities are now seeking Malibu private detective James Rockford."

Rockford snaps to attention.

Reporter: "whose missing '79 tan Firebird was used in the defection and whose Malibu office and residence were the scene of a shootout in the early morning hours. And, in all of this, what of the Kirovs? Talented, fragile performers from another land, lost and now perhaps dead because of desperate attempt to gain freedom."

Rockford could just cry.

Not sure what to make of his predicament, Rockford turns to his father for help.

Rocky: "I thought you was up there fishing. Instead you're messing around with Russians, arranging defections."

Rockford: "I was fishing."

Rocky: "Sonny, you never used to lie to me—and I don't think this here is the time to start."

Rockford: "Dad, I didn't kidnap the Kirovs. I wouldn't know a ballet dancer from a plate of eggs."

Rocky: "I had the FBI talking to me half the night."

Rockford: "I just wish I know where my car was. Maybe there's some prints on it, some piece of evidence that would clear me."

Rockford's car, it turns out, has been ditched in a bad neighborhood—and stolen by a pair of tough-looking Chicano kids.

Rocky, meanwhile, has convinced his son to go to the police. He drives Rockford to headquarters. Inside, it's all hustle and bustle—cops, feds, Soviet agents and newspaper reporters running every which way. They're all working on the Rockford-Kirov case.

Overheard: "Tell you guys I want this guy, Rockford. I want him 10 minutes ago!"

"The Russian people will have the opportunity to question him first. We will take him to our embassy. Russian nationals are involved!"

"We catch this slug P.I., ...we're gonna hang by his toes. He won't see daylight for 50 years!"

Even Lieutenant Chapman is hollering: "Look, I don't want to hear excuses. You pick this jerk Rockford up. At last, I got him where I want him!"

Naturally, Rockford turns tail and runs.

A news report on television: "A strange twist in the Kirov defection or kidnapping occurred late this afternoon. A car traced to Malibu private investigator James Rockford and used in the possible Kirov kidnapping was also the getaway vehicle in an East Los Angeles holdup this afternoon. Authorities are pondering the possible connection of this holdup with the defection or kidnapping of Anton and Nina Kirov."

The only angle that Rockford can think to pursue is questioning Marty Boxx, who according to news reports refused to explain his involvement in the Kirov case.

Rockford—wearing a sluggo cap, dark glasses and a tweed jacket—heads to the Boxx Agency. Inside he tries to run one on Boxx's secretary.

Rockford: "Mr. Jerome Alexander of Creative Celebrity Management here to see Mr. Boxx about Mr. Nicholson's contract."

It turns out that Angel Martin is there, still playing Hollywood agent, and he sees some character down the hall dickering with the secretary. Because of Rockford's disguise, Angel doesn't recognize him from behind. Angel decides to give the guy a hard time.

Angel: "Hey, you! Yeah, you, with the polo hat. This is top management here. Handlers and schmiklers deal with the Boxx Boys on the third floor. You got that?"

Rockford turns. He's fuming.

Angel: "Jimmy?"

Angel turns to run. "No calls or appointments."

Rockford catches him and shoves him around a little.

Rockford: "I should've known you were messed up in this somehow."

Angel: "Jimmy. Jimmy. Don't, Jimmy. Don't. Don't. Look, this is the best deal I ever ran into. I got Marty Boxx on the hook. If I talk he's implicated in the Kirov thing. He gave me this office. I get to beat up on people, blow deals, cause trouble. And, Jimmy, I get 10 percent of Marty's 10 percent."

Rockford: "Start talking."

Angel: "Okay, okay. Look, Jimmy. My windpipe. I got a sensitive windpipe."

Rockford: "You stole my car, right? Let's start there."

Angel: "Stole? Jimmy. A little loan. A little help that one gives to another. You were out of town so I—borrowed."

Rockford: "Do you borrow it often, Angel?"

Angel:"Well, Jimmy. Depends what you call often."

Rockford: "Did you use it last August?

Angel: "August? August? It's a long time back."

Rockford: "I came back from that case in Toronto and it was over 10,000 miles, so I missed my warranty checkup. I accused Dad of using it, almost ruined our relationship. You were there. Remember? He stomped out of the trailer."

Angel: "Oh, yeah. I think I may have."

Rockford: "You put a thousand miles on it."

Angel: "Not me, Jimmy. Eddie Whitefeather did that. I never figured, when I sublet it to Eddie, that he was gonna take it to Tijuana for the weekend. He's the one that ticked that mileage off. Why don't you talk to him?"

Rockford: "Do you hate me? Have I done anything to make you hate me?"

Angel: "Naw, Jimmy. Nothing like that. It's just—well, do you want to hear the truth? You're a pigeon. Your sense of friendship is as easy to hit as a dump truck. You should've hit me half-a-dozen times over the years but you never do.

You're a soft touch."

Rockford punches Angel in the stomach.

Rockford gets the rest of the lowdown from Angel and then off they go to Marty Boxx's place. When Rockford gets his mitts on Marty, he's as rough with him as he was earlier with Angel. And like Angel before him, Marty is quick to start spilling it.

Rockford: "You were planning the defection. Who knew?"

Boxx: "The two Jerrys knew and Marty and, of course, Mr. Martain here. And Ty."

Rockford: "Who's Ty?"

Angel: "He's the chauffeur. He's the one who didn't show up. That's why I ended up driving the car."

Rockford: "The chauffeur? That's classic. In nine out of 10 mob hits, the chauffeur is the finger man."

Rockford's piecing it all together now.

Rockford learns that Ty Andrews is a down-on-his-luck actor. Rockford and Angel head to the actor's home. Outside Andrews' home, located on a dead-end street, Rockford spots the actor—a man we recognize as one of the gunmen who menaced Angel and took the Kirovs. Rockford tells Angel to take the car and get help.

Rockford stays behind to keep an eye on the house as Angel drives away—the wrong way, toward the dead end. So Angel mindlessly turns around and picks a driveway at random, which happens to be the very house that Rockford's staking out. Rockford tries to stop Angel from heading to the front door but he's not fast enough. Ty and his cohort are standing in the doorway.

Ty: "It's the guy from the trailer."

A scuffle ensues, in which Rockford does all the damage. Inside, after Rockford ties up the kidnappers, they find the Kirovs bound and gagged.

Angel: "Anton, Nina, allow me to introduce myself. I'm Marty Martain of Martain's Creative Talent Celebrity Artists Management Agency. What I have here (holding a blank sheet of paper) is an unwritten letter of agreement. A simple little seven-year contract. We'll fill in the details later."

Back at Rockford's place—his bullet-ridden and stripped-down car out front—Rockford, Rocky and Angel are watching the latest TV news report on the Kirov case.

Rocky: "Well, it comes out pretty good, all things considered."

Rockford: "Yeah, if you don't count the damage to my car."

Angel: "Hell, Jimmy. Forget that pile of junk. Look, you come into the Jerry Martin Agency, we can set you up in a little office. You can deal with the little clients. I'll teach you the rap."

Rockford: "You just don't learn, do you, Angel?"

Angel: "Learn, learn, that's all I been doing is learning. I'm booking a few really hot C-and-W acts, Jimmy. I put Mel Tillis into the Palomino for three nights and (the Boxx Agency didn't) even handle Mel Tillis. And I got five grand down up front.

"I call it Ernest and Andy money. I told the club, 'No dough, no show.' They came across like six peanut vendors fighting for a corner. I put five grand in my poke and ol' Mel Tillis is down at the club trying to straighten it out with the booking agent. I'm out of it. I mean, how is that for smooth?"

Rockford: "It's crooked. It'll catch up with you."

Angel: "How's it gonna catch up with me, hunh? How? You tell me. How?"

As he's saying this, there's a knock on the door. Angel gets to his feet to answer it. The man outside turns out to be Mel Tillis. And, boy, is he ever steamed!

CHAPTER NINETEEN:

ODDS AND ENDS

Ours is an age of trivial pursuits and television offers an endless supply of information toward that end. One simply can't watch a TV series for a number of years without picking up a few tidbits of insignifia along the way. These odds and ends may be of no particular value in knowing, yet they are locked away in our brains nonetheless.

The Rockford Files is no exception. As James Garner once noted of this aspect of the show: "There are some people in this country who know every phone number—every license plate on the show. If I use a wrong license or say a wrong number, I get piles of letters."

That being the case, let's take a look at some more notable bits of trivia regarding Jim Rockford and his friends.

ROCKFORD'S VITAL STATISTICS

Physically, James Garner and Jim Rockford were virtually one and the same: In 1974, when the series began production, Garner was listed in his studio biography as 6 feet, 3 inches, 190 pounds. (Two hundred pounds and 6-foot-2 were more accurate figures.)

Rockford, meanwhile, was listed in an early episode at 6-foot-1, 195 pounds. A year later, when described in an all points bulletin, he was "approximately 6 feet, 2 inches, 200 pounds."

Also like Garner, who underwent three knee operations during the series ' six-year run, Rockford had bad wheels too. In one episode, when roughed up by a cop, Rockford complained, "Come on, I don't have shin guards on—and I got bad knees."

ROCKFORD'S PAST

Rockford served five years in San Quentin for a robbery he didn't commit. He was sentenced to 20 years to life but received a full pardon from the governor when new evidence cleared his name.

ROCKFORD'S HOME

Rockford's home and office was a mobile home on the beach. Originally it was located at 2354 Pacific Coast Highway in Los Angeles, but later he lived at 29 Cove Road (in the Paradise Cove Trailer Colony) in Malibu.

Curiously, his Yellow Pages ad gives yet another address: "The Rockford Agency. Our trained investigators have specialized in CLOSED CASES since 1968. CRIMINAL ONLY. 24-hour service. Licensed and Bonded. 24 Ocean Blvd., Los Angeles."

Given the conflicting addresses, our suggestion is to contact him by telephone and leave a message on his answering machine.

"This is Jim Rockford. At the tone leave your name and message. I'll get back to you." His phone number: (213)-555-2368 Or is it 555-9000? He's used that one before too.

ROCKFORD'S CAR

Rockford drove a gold Pontiac Firebird, California license plate number OKG-853. Rockford's remarkable driving ability was a trait that Garner shared, as well. Garner, who did much of his own stunt driving during the series, has long had a passion for auto racing.

In the 1960s he established the American International Racing Corporation and at one point owned 17 race cars and had a half dozen drivers under contract. He did his own driving in *Grand Prix*, a 1966 motion picture, and in 1970 he placed second in the 1970 Baja California road race. Garner even drove the pace car at the Indianapolis 500 in 1975 and 1979.

ET CETERA

Like Garner, Rockford served in the Army in Korea. Rockford was a corporal.

Rocky drove a four-wheel-drive pick-up, California plate number 1C02677.

Rocky's address: 3654 Willowcrest Drive, Santa Monica, CA 90406.

Angel lived at the Hotel Edison.

Boring, But Necessary Ordering Information!

Payment:
All orders must be prepaid by check or money order. Do not send cash. All payments must be made in US funds only.

Shipping:
We offer several methods of shipment for our product. Sometimes a book can be delayed if we are temporarily out of stock. You should note on your order whether you prefer us to ship the book as soon as available or send you a merchandise credit good for other goodies or send you your money back immediately.

Postage is as follows:

Normal Post Office: For books priced under $10.00—for the first book add $2.50. For each additional book under $10.00 add $1.00. (This is per indidividual book priced under $10.00. Not the order total.) For books priced over $10.00—for the first book add $3.25. For each additional book over $10.00 add $2.00.(This is per individual book priced over $10.00, not the order total.) These orders are filled as quickly as possible. Shipments normally take 2 or 3 weeks, but allow up to 12 weeks for delivery.

Special UPS 2 Day Blue Label Rush Service or Priority Mail(Our Choice). Special service is available for desperate Couch Potatoes. These books are shipped within 24 hours of when we receive the order and should normally take 2 to 3 days to get from us to you. For the first RUSH SERVICE book under $10.00 add $5.00. For each additional 1 book under $10.00 add $1.75. (This is per individual book priced under $10.00, not the order total.) For the first RUSH SERVICE book over $10.00 add $7.00 For each additional book over $10.00 add $4.00 per book.(This is per individual book priced over $10.00, not the order total.)

Canadian shipping rates add 20% to the postage total.
Foreign shipping rates add 50% to the postage total.
All Canadian and foreign orders are shipped either book or printed matter.
Rush Service is not available.

DISCOUNTS!DISCOUNTS!
Because your orders keep us in business we offer a discount to people that buy a lot of our books as our way of saying thanks. On orders over $25,00 we give a 5% discount. On orders over $50.00 we give a 10% discount. On orders over $100.00 we give a 15% discount. On orders over over $150.00 we giver a 20 % discount.

Please list alternates when possible.

Please state if you wish a refund or for us to backorder an item if it is not in stock.

100% satisfaction guaranteed.
We value your support. You will receive a full refund as long as the copy of the book you are not happy with is received back by us in reasonable condition. No questions asked, except we would like to know how we failed you. Refunds and credits are given as soon as we receive back the item you do not want.

Please have mercy on Phyllis and carefully fill out this form in the neatest way you can. Remember, she has to read a lot of them every day and she wants to get it right and keep you happy! You may use a duplicate of this order blank as long as it is clear. Please don't forget to include payment! And remember, we love repeat friends.

MORE COUPON PAGE

_____Batman And Robin Serials $16.95

_____The Complete Batman And Robin Serials $19.95

_____The Green Hornet Serials $16.95

_____The Flash Gordon Serials Part 1 $16.95

_____The Flash Gordon Serials Part 2 $16.95

_____The Shadow Serials $16.95

_____Blackhawk Serials $16.95

_____Serial Adventures $14.95   ISBN#1-55698-236-4

_____Trek: The Lost Years $12.95   ISBN#1-55698-220-8

_____The Trek Encyclopedia $19.95   ISBN#1-55698-205-4

_____The Trek Crew Book $9.95   ISBN#1-55698-257-7

_____The Making Of The Next Generation $14.95   ISBN# 1-55698-219-4

_____The Complete Guide To The Next Generation $19.95

_____The Best Of Enterprise Incidents: The Magazine For Star Trek Fans $9.95
                                   ISBN# 1-55698-231-3

_____The Gunsmoke Years $14.95   ISBN# 1-55698-221-6

_____The Wild Wild West Book $14.95   ISBN# 1-55698-162-7

_____Who Was That Masked Man $14.95   ISBN#1-55698-227-5

NAME:_____

STREET:_____

CITY:_____

STATE:_____

ZIP:_____

TOTAL:_____ SHIPPING_____

SEND TO: Couch Potato, Inc. 5715 N. Balsam Rd., Las Vegas, NV 89130